Praise for

Quarter-Acre of Heartache

"*Quarter-Acre of Heartache*'s blend of autobiography, cultural memory, and oral history crafts a timely reminder of the power of indigenous resistance."

ELLERY THOMAS LEARY, Historian, Archeologist; M.A., University College London

"I am happy that *Quarter-Acre of Heartache* was translated into Russian in 1994 and is being republished in English for the crucial year of 2026, when America will celebrate its 250th anniversary. American Indians and the indigenous peoples of the Russian North, the Khanty and Mansi, are close in their mentality and history. Brother Wolf and Brother Tree, truth and respect, these values are of a different order than the power of capital, and bring our peoples together."

MARINA AYPINA, editor, Bulletin of the Assembly of Representatives of Indigenous Minorities of the North, Khanty-Mansiysk Region, Siberia

"This book is a testament to the persistent injustice Americans have served up to Native Americans. It's also a witness to the reality that democracy can be used to disempower outsiders. Smith's presentation enables the reader to hear directly the voice of this proud, courageous, clear-sighted, and stubborn Golden Hill Paugussett Indian chief who took a stand in twentieth century Connecticut against three hundred years of abuse to his people."

JENNY RABODZEENKO, Ph.D., Cultural Anthropologist; Shikaakwa, Miami-Illinois land

Quarter-Acre of Heartache

Claude Clayton Smith

SHANTI ARTS PUBLISHING
BRUNSWICK, MAINE

QUARTER-ACRE OF HEARTACHE

Published by Shanti Arts LLC, 193 Hillside Road,
Brunswick, Maine 04011; shantiarts.com
First published by Pocahontas Press, 1985

Designed by Shanti Arts Designs
Front cover image by Bart Levy
Maps by Jacqueline P. Read

Printed in the United States of America

ISBN: 978-1-962082-71-6 (softcover)
ISBN: 978-1-962082-73-0 (ebook)

Library of Congress Control Number (LCCN): 2025938359

In memoriam:

Aurelius Piper, Chief Big Eagle

1916–2008

CONTENTS

.

ACKNOWLEDGMENTS

A 1979 report titled "American Indians in Connecticut: Past to Present," prepared for the Connecticut Indian Affairs Council (CIAC) by Mary E. Guillette, was helpful to me in the early stages of this book, although Chief Big Eagle disputed the accuracy of some of its details. The report was subsequently revised.

The photographs in *Quarter-Acre of Heartache* vary in quality. Some were reproduced from black-and-white snapshots, color snapshots, or newsprint. Others I took myself. Many photos that would have been of interest were confiscated by officials from available files during investigations of Chief Big Eagle. I wish to thank *The Trumbull Times*, *The Bridgeport Post*, *The Connecticut Post*, *The Milford Citizen*, *The Shelton Herald*, and *The New York Times* for their interest and assistance.

To give dignity to a man is above all things.

—Chief Sitting Bull

PREFACE

to the

SECOND EDITION

WHEN I WAS A YOUNG BOY growing up in Stratford, Connecticut, my father often took me fishing, together with my brother and grandfather, to Lake Zoar In Southbury. We would rent a rowboat from a man named Burns Ingraham, who lived in an old cottage on a hillside along the lake. Burns Ingraham was a full-blooded Sioux Indian. I remember him as a large, silent man with fine lines cross-hatching the ruddy skin of his face and neck. He had made the rowboats we rented all by himself.

One day Burns Ingraham invited my grandfather to go hunting. "I don't have a license," my grandfather objected. "Never use one," Burns Ingraham replied flatly. So the two of them went off hunting, Burns Ingraham shot a deer, and a game warden arrested my grandfather.

"Indians don't need a license," my grandfather later explained, "because the woods is theirs anyway!"

That lesson stuck in my mind. Certain people had been around for so long that they held a special claim to the land.

But such distant experiences only served to raise questions. What was an Indian doing in Connecticut? Didn't Indians belong out West? The only Indians I had studied in school were those who had helped the Pilgrims with the first Thanksgiving. After that, they seemed to have disappeared.

It was not until I began research for my historical novel *The*

Stratford Devil (Shanti Arts, 2023; Pocahontas Press, 2007; Walker & Company, 1984) that I came to realize the sad truth about America's Indians, our native Americans whose struggles are far from over. *Quarter-Acre of Heartache* documents those struggles by focusing on a present-day, real-life descendant of the Indians that appear in *The Stratford Devil*—Aurelius Piper, Chief Big Eagle, of the Paugussett Indian nation.

In 1925, at the age of nine, Mr. Piper ran away from the Golden Hill Indian Reservation in Trumbull, Connecticut, for a life in the woods of Maine. In 1973 he returned to fight against the legal termination of his tribe and to protect the land of his ancestors against blatant encroachment. In the process, he converted one of the oldest (1659) and smallest (1/4 acre) continuous reservations in America into an internationally known "living museum" of Native American culture.

Chief Big Eagle is at once a compassionate and controversial individual. He has been honored by the Milford, Connecticut, police department for his work with children in that town. He once granted the wish of a terminally ill New Jersey boy by literally giving him the shirt off his back. Yet this same man was accused of arson on the Golden Hill Reservation and blamed for the much-publicized slayings of black youths in Atlanta. The former case was never solved. The latter ended with the conviction of Wayne B. Williams.

Both the compassion and controversy stem, I feel, from the fact that Chief Big Eagle has been willing to fight for the Paugussett people—for their right to survive and to lead a decent life. The people of Trumbull have either been for the Chief or against him. There appears to be no middle ground. But in the unbiased eyes of the law, after court battles lasting more than a decade, Chief Big Eagle has been vindicated.

Quarter-Acre of Heartache tells the story of Chief Big Eagle and the Golden Hill Indians of the Paugussett Indian nation. Past and present, it is a tale of harassment and bloodshed. William Kunstler, the noted civil rights attorney, has supported the legal effort of the tribe, and the reservation itself was defended in a showdown by Clyde Bellecourt and Russell Means, activists of the American

Indian Movement (AIM) who occupied Wounded Knee against the FBI in 1973.

I have chosen to write in the first person, in the voice of Chief Big Eagle as I have come to know it, to let the Chief speak for himself. For, as the federally chartered American Indian Policy Review Committee has concluded, "Only the Indians themselves can tell the real story."

I wish to thank Mr. Piper for his time and patience, for the hours of tape recording, for providing access to the reservation archives and artifacts, and for reading the drafts of this manuscript as they were written. Most of all, I wish to thank him for an education that would have otherwise eluded me.

I hope this book will help locate the struggles of today's Native Americans at their point of origin in the East, in the context of modern suburbia, where they have been going on in the back yard all along.

Shawsville, Virginia
August 1985

AT AN INTERNATIONAL CONFERENCE IN OHIO in October 1989, I presented a copy of the first edition of this book to Alexander Vashchenko, the Soviet authority on Native American literature and folklore, then a research professor at the A. M. Gorky Institute of World Literature in Moscow. Chief Big Eagle had signed the title page with a lavish statement about our two nations "walking in peace." Thrilled with the gift, Vashchenko read it overnight and announced in the morning that he wanted to translate it into Russian. As he later wrote to me, "*Quarter-Acre of Heartache* will be translated by me and published by Friendship of Peoples in 1992, to commemorate—and argue—the Indians' point of view of the quincentenary of Columbus's discovery of America. We plan to do it as part (final and crucial) of the long story of Indian testimonials: Black Elk's, Chief Joseph's, Geronimo's. So the book is going to be thick. But then I will see that it is published separately also" (see page 160).

In addition to this announcement, Vashchenko invited Chief Big Eagle and me to visit Russia that summer. Three weeks later the Berlin Wall fell and the Soviet Union descended into chaos. Nonetheless, the Chief and I ventured to Moscow and Leningrad in 1990 and returned the following summer for the 11th annual powwow of the Indianists, Russian citizens who have dedicated their lives to the preservation of Native American culture and traditions, a quasi-illegal organization according to Article 227 of the Russian code, which prohibits all activity of "reactionary content."

These dramatic experiences resulted in another book—*Red Men in Red Square* (Pocahontas Press, 1994), my account of Chief Big Eagle's interactions with the Indianists, including one Native Siberian—a symbolic reunion of ancient peoples, East and West.

Chief Big Eagle passed away in August of 2008 at the age of ninety-two. I learned of his death when contacted for a comment by a reporter from the Washington Bureau of *The Connecticut Post*, which subsequently published a lengthy article on the Chief's legacy. *The New York Times* followed suit with an extensive obituary and photograph (see pages 158–159). The Chief's son Little Eagle, a toddler during the war for the quarter-acre, and his sister

White Fawn, who was three at the time, appear in this edition of *Quarter-Acre of Heartache*, as they did in the first, in a loving family photograph, together with the Chief and his fourth wife, Marsha (see page 117). Today, Little Eagle (I-Hahm-Tet) lives on his father's land in Maine, and White Fawn (Waupatuquay), now Clan Mother of the Golden Hill Tribe of the Paugussett nation, lives with her mother on the reservation in Trumbull, carrying on the work of her father by pursuing federal recognition for her tribe (see photo on page 161).

In 2026, as Americans grapple with the true meaning of our country's 250th birthday, the Paugussetts will observe the 50th anniversary of the start of the war that threatened the termination of their reservation and very existence of their tribe. Meanwhile, the plight of what Chief Big Eagle called "Indian Country" is being kept in the public consciousness as never before. Films such as *Fancy Dance* and *Killers of the Flower Moon*, starring Academy Award nominee Lily Gladstone, continue to call attention to Missing and Murdered Indigenous Women (MMIW), while the documentary *Sugarcane* explores the tragedy of Indian "boarding schools" meant to strip Native children of their language, culture, and identity.

On a different note, Indian Country has applauded the fact that President Biden, before leaving office, commuted the sentence of eighty-year-old Leonard Peltier, the North Dakota Chippewa imprisoned for nearly fifty years in connection with the murder of two FBI agents in a 1975 confrontation on the Pine Ridge Indian Reservation. On February 18, 2025, Peltier—long an international *cause célèbre*—was released from incarceration in Florida and returned to family and friends for "home containment" at North Dakota's Turtle Mountain Indian Reservation, near Belcourt, North Dakota, where he was born.

Chief Big Eagle had visited Peltier in 1985, after the latter was transferred to Leavenworth from prison in Marion, Illinois. During that visit he presented Peltier with a beaded belt he had made, bearing the same face as seen on T-shirts stating FREE LEONARD PELTIER. When the Chief and I were in Russia in 1990, the Indianists asked me to carry home a petition for executive clemency on behalf of Peltier and forward it to the chairman of the

Senate Committee on Indian Affairs. Although I readily assented, the request frightened me, due to the uncertain legal status of the Indianist movement; but Vashchenko, who'd asked me to smuggle home a painting for a colleague as well (Russian artwork was not to leave the country), escorted us through Customs at Sheremeteyevo Airport in Moscow without incident.

The timing of this new edition of *Quarter-Acre of Heartache* is ironic. Most Americans know 1620 as the year the Pilgrims arrived in Massachusetts on the *Mayflower*. Most don't know, however, that the ruthless Pequots, who were feared by the Whites as well as all Connecticut tribes, were destroyed in 1637 to clear the way for progressive settlement. Two years later my home town of Stratford was founded on the banks of the Housatonic River. The land known today as Trumbull—the permanent, modern site of the Golden Hill Paugussett Indian Nation—was initially North Stratford, becoming its own entity in the late eighteenth century.

In telling the story of Native Americans in Connecticut, history seems to have conspired to unfold in terms of centuries. The last-ditch attempt of colonial-era Indians to rid themselves of White invaders was called King Philip's War. It was led by Metacom of the Narragansett tribe, whom the English called King Philip. The fighting lasted from 1675 to 1676, ending with a massacre in a battle at Mystic, Connecticut. A century later came the American Revolution and the Declaration of Independence. And two centuries after that, at the height of the American Bicentennial in July of 1976, what Chief Big Eagle called "the war for the quarter-acre" began when the tribe was threatened by a lawsuit, challenging its claim to its reservation land. Subsequent events, as recounted in this edition, secured the legal status of the reservation in perpetuity.

Now, in 2025, in the face of America's 250th birthday—call it what you will, the Sestercentennial, Bisesqicentennial, or Quarter Millennial—the Golden Hill Paugussetts are celebrating half a century of peace with a party of their own.

—Madison, Wisconsin
April 2025

Having succeeded his Uncle Chief Black Hawk as leader of the Golden Hill Indians, Chief Big Eagle sits on the quarter-acre reservation in 1974, at the beginning of a decade of legal struggles with the state of Connecticut and neighbors of Trumbull. Credit: Eddie Hausner/The New York Times, Redux

PART I

CHAPTER ONE

MY NAME IS AURELIUS PIPER. I was born in 1916, three hundred years too late for the kind of life I would like to have lived. A way of life that is no longer possible. The way of my ancestors.

I am a Native American. I wear my hair in twin braids tied with strips of rawhide. I wear an eagle feather in the band of my flat-brimmed hat. In recent years I have had to carry a gun for my own protection.

I want to explain about that.

It is a long and often complicated story, so please be patient. The hurried hunter finds no deer. Many little steps make a journey.

I live in one of the wealthiest suburbs in the United States, in a section of Trumbull, Connecticut, known as Nichols. It is a very fine place for White people, a very lovely New England town. Stone walls line the woods and fields. There are village greens, old churches with tall steeples, and saltbox houses with wooden shingles. The people who live here are well-educated and successful.

I like to sit on the front porch of my little log house and watch the traffic on the Shelton Road. Every morning the school buses go by among the automobiles commuting to Bridgeport. Trailer trucks rumble through too, carrying goods to the malls and shopping centers. Every now and then a long station wagon, driven by a well-dressed White woman, pulls into the Chevron station across the street, ringing a bell as it hits the snake-like hose. Later in the day station wagons like this will carry the neighborhood children to piano lessons and horseback riding.

Not far away, new housing developments are being cut into the mountain laurel and white oak of the Connecticut countryside. None of the handsome houses, when finished, will sell for less than one hundred thousand dollars. Many will cost as much as three hundred thousand. (In December 2024, the median cost of a home in Trumbull was six hundred and fifty thousand dollars. —Editor) Trumbull is a very fine place for White people. It has not been a very good place for Indians.

Busloads of school children have come from all over, at all times, to this log house. Often, while sitting on the front porch and waiting for the buses to arrive, I think of things to explain to the children so they can learn to judge what is real and not real, so they can come to know the truth about Indians. For if the youngest children walk in truth, they will grow up in the truth. Then the truth will be known. The truth will prevail.

The mailboxes I can see from my front porch remind me of the bread-loaf-shaped wigwams of my ancestors. That is where my story begins, with my ancestors.

•

For ten thousand years the Native American people from whom I am descended have inhabited these New England regions. They were called *Indians* by the European explorers who felt they had found their way to India. The name has stuck. But my ancestors were not *Indians*. They were *Native Americans*. The *very first* Americans.

They came as wandering hunters from the north and west. They roamed the wide valleys that were formed as the glaciers of the Ice Age receded. They came to the east, the Land of the Rising Sun.

The earth here at that time was tundra—covered with lichens, mosses, and stunted shrubs. But over hundreds of years, the cone-bearing trees grew up—pine, hemlock, and spruce. Then came the trees we know today—oak, birch, and ash—trees that lose their leaves each year.

My ancestors lived by hunting wild game in the woodlands and meadows and by fishing in the rivers and streams. They were handsome people—short by today's standards, but lean and strong, with dark hair, dark eyes, dark skin. Over the years they learned to till the soil, bringing corn, beans, and squash from the earth.

Most of the vegetables produced in America today were originally raised by my ancestors before Columbus arrived. Potatoes, corn, even chili peppers. The Native Americans taught the White Man how to grow them.

My ancestors also made medicines from over two hundred plants. They used every part of the plant, from root to leaf. They developed cures for illnesses, sores, and wounds of all kinds.

Of course, since they didn't know how to write, they left no written records of their civilization. But their ancient burial mounds show evidence of cremation—the burning of corpses. Such a practice suggests respect for the dead. Hence, respect for life. Respect for life is something we must never forget. Respect for all living things.

Many of the tools my ancestors used were destroyed over thousands of years by the acid-like Connecticut soil. Other tools were lost because of the clumsy methods of the archaeologists who studied them, hoping to learn about the past. What a shame! There is a simple beauty to the relics that have been saved—the bone knives, stone axes, clay pots.

Many farmers who have farmed this land in Nichols have found some very important Indian artifacts. They have them in their homes today. Some of the farmers have more artifacts than I do because they have more land. The artifacts help you to imagine the life that my ancestors led.

It was very different from life today. It was a life determined by the passing of the seasons.

In summer settlements, my ancestors tended to their crops. They lived in wigwams they made by stretching hides and bark across bent poles. After the harvest in the fall, they moved inland to hunt. They spent the winter in temporary villages set in protected valleys where they lived on dried foods and stored nuts. In the spring, they moved to fishing camps along the rivers and the Connecticut coast.

And they drank only water until the White Man came. Think of that! No milk, Kool-Aid, or Coca-Cola. Just pure, clean water.

The clothing of my ancestors was simple—animal skins, furs, and leggings in winter; loincloths, skirts, and shirts in summer; moccasins always on the feet. They rubbed oil and fat into their skin for warmth and protection from insects. They decorated their bodies with paint and tattoos. They wore shells and beads on their arms and necks.

And until the White Man came, my ancestors were the dominant people in southwest *quinnehtukqut*—the land *beside the long tidal river*. That is how Connecticut got its name.

The Connecticut River is the largest in New England. It flows for three hundred and fifty miles from New Hampshire to Long Island Sound. Until the White Man came, the Connecticut River Valley must have been a paradise. My ancestors walked in beauty.

My ancestors were the five tribes of the Paugussett nation, a group of blood-related clans. At one time they controlled half a million acres in southwest Connecticut—from New Haven to Fairfield along the coast, to the north of Woodbury and Danbury. Records show that relatives of the Paugussetts were living in Farmington too. Other records show that the tribe held a narrow strip of land that extended as far north as Norfolk, almost to the Massachusetts line. Half a million acres to roam in peace.

The five tribes of the Paugussett nation took their names from the features of the territory they occupied. The Pootatucks lived by *the falls river*, today known as the Housatonic. The Pequannocks lived in a *cleared field* in Bridgeport. The Naugatucks lived by *a single tree*. There is a town called Naugatuck today. The Wepawaugs lived in Milford. Their name means *river* or *reservoir*. And the Paugussetts lived along the shores of the Housatonic River *at the narrows* or *crossing place*. They gave their name to the entire group of tribes.

The Paugussett confederacy. My ancestors.

CHAPTER TWO

MY ANCESTORS FEARED NO ONE, not even the ruthless Pequots to the east. Swift messengers carried the news from village to village. They traveled on foot or by dugout canoe. Each tribe spoke a dialect of the Algonquian tongue. Their *sachems*—or chiefs—listened carefully to the advice of the *sagamores*—or lesser chiefs—and braves. The *sachem* was entrusted with the sacred property of his tribe—the symbolic headdress and the belts of *wampumpeag*.

Tribal leaders were always men, but women had their share of power too. Indian squaws are often pictured walking behind their men as if they were slaves. The squaws carried the blankets and food and utensils. But there were not slaves. They carried these things because they owned them. The women owned all the things that were necessary for the tribe to survive.

We hear a lot today about women's liberation. In a way it is as old as my ancestors.

At tribal councils, when a decision could not be reached unanimously, it was the Clan Mother who made the final decision. It was the Clan Mother who selected the next chief. I know about that because I was selected by the Clan Mother known as Rising Star. She chose me to walk the path of my uncle, Chief Black Hawk, who died in 1974.

I am a thirty-generation descendant of the Pequannock tribe of the Paugussett nation. I am Aurelius Piper, Chief Big Eagle.

Now you know why I am so concerned about my ancestors. It is my responsibility to protect them. To preserve their culture as best I can.

But my neighbors do not like it when I beat my drum. They say my drumming is a lot of noise. To me, this drumming is the heartbeat of my ancestors.

The drum is made from the bark of our Brother-the-Tree. It is made from the hide of our Brother-the-Deer. The drum is in the shape of a circle. The circle represents the Center of Life, a life of balance and equality. My ancestors lived within the Circle by telling the truth and understanding the land, by answering the Creator's call to each new day. The drum is a reminder of the life my ancestors led.

It was a very peaceful life, a quiet life of hunting and fishing. In those days there were plenty of deer and turkeys in the forest, plenty of perch and bass in the lakes and streams, plenty of clams and mussels along the coast.

My ancestors were skilled with their hands. They turned wood, hides, bones, and clay into the tools of daily life. They made mats and baskets from cornstalks and leaves.

And at mid-summer, when the green corn was ripe, they held a ceremony to give thanks to the Creator. Because corn nourished both body and spirit. Because corn made life possible. There was corn meal for eating, corn cobs for scrubbing, and cornstalks and leaves for weaving. It was necessary to thank the Creator or famine and hardship would follow.

My ancestors thanked the Creator at ceremonies throughout the year—at the planting and again at the harvest. There were ceremonies for the sun and moon and thunder too. My ancestors believed in many guiding spirits. All were thanked in turn so harmony would follow.

My ancestors led a life without warfare. Now and then, there was fighting with the tribes of other nations, but both sides went home as soon as the mission was accomplished. Such fighting was necessary to maintain respect.

The real trouble was not between Native Americans. The real trouble began when the White Man came.

What happened when the White Man came?

Nothing at first. Because the first White men—the bearded Vikings who reached the east coast of America in the fifteenth century—came only to explore, to look around. They came and went without leaving their mark.

But the White men that followed—the Dutch and then the English—came to stay.

One reason was the fur trade. The Indians along the coast could get animal pelts from the inland tribes and trade them to the White Man for precious goods. The White Man had metals—copper, brass, and iron—that the Indians had never seen before. The metals could be used for better weapons and tools. And the White Man had cloth and blankets, so much finer than animal hides.

Wampumpeag, called *wampum* for short, was also an item of trade. Wampum consisted of strings of purple and white quahog shells. Clam shells. My ancestors used them as ornaments. Wampum was hung on belts and straps. It was a status symbol. It was used instead of money in the fur trade.

And the Dutch soon learned the score. Metal and cloth meant wampum from the Indians on the coast. Wampum meant furs from the Indians who hunted inland. Furs meant great riches in Europe.

But the White Man was greedy for wampum and greedy for land. He encroached on the Indian territories. He had no respect for the idea that the land was to be used, not taken or bought and sold.

So my ancestors carried out raids against the White Man. To protect the land. To gain respect. There is that word again. *Respect.* It is one of the values we teach to Indian children. The word has gone out of style, but it must be preserved.

CHAPTER THREE

INDIANS HAVE A SPECIAL RECIPE that we share among ourselves. It is a recipe for dog head stew. The recipe makes enough for fifty people:

Carefully prepare one medium-size dog head. Remove teeth from jaw and bone and set aside for future use. Remove the hair and save it too. Into kettle add heaping handfuls of camos bulbs and cattail roots. The eggs from two medium-size salmon may be combined with water. Cover, place over fire, and bring to a slow boil for three hours.

It is customary to observe the rites of preparation in order to have all present appreciate the dish that will begin the feast. At the proper moment, using the ceremonial arrow, impale the dog head and bring it forth for all to observe the excellence of the dish. Then allow fifteen minutes for all White people to excuse themselves and leave for home. Bury stew in back yard and bring forth the roasted turkey with all the trimmings. The others have been invited to the feast. The fact that they didn't stay is their own tough luck.

This recipe, of course, is a joke. It is a way for Indians to deal with the mistaken idea that we eat dogs. It is sad that such a joke exists, because Indians do not eat dogs. Such mistaken ideas must be corrected.

But I was talking about what happened to my ancestors when the White Man came:

The White Man caused two big problems. Double trouble, like the forked tongue of a poisonous snake. Dissension and disease. Squabbling and sickness.

The disease came first. Smallpox and measles. Today they are no problem. But in the sixteenth century, when these diseases reached America for the first time, they killed more than one quarter of the native population. In the early seventeenth century, further epidemics were responsible for the deaths of ninety percent of the remaining Indian population. Entire villages were wiped out or abandoned. The losses sapped the strength and spirit of those who survived.

By the time the Pilgrims arrived in Massachusetts in the year 1620, the native population of America—which had once numbered nearly one hundred thousand—had been reduced by disease to just a few thousand. Still, the Indians greatly outnumbered the Whites. It would have been easy for them to drive the White Man out. But my ancestors could not get organized because of the dissension, the squabbling among the tribes.

The White Man learned to *divide and conquer*. He turned tribe against tribe. The separate Indian nations competed for the White Man's trade and protection. The White Man offered precious goods. His *firesticks* were more powerful than my ancestors' bows and arrows.

The Dutch trappers and traders were followed by English settlers. And these new White men thought of the Indians in a strange way—as godless children of the Devil. The White Man tried to give his religion to the Indians, to make the Indians in his own image. Those that didn't accept it were eliminated. Exterminated. The White Man tried to make the Indian extinct. And his religion gave him a good excuse.

Extinct. That is not too strong a word. The dinosaur is extinct. Soon the wolf will be extinct too. But there is a difference. The White Man did not make the dinosaur extinct. But he will make the wolf extinct. Just like he tried to make the Indian extinct.

He began with the Pequots.

The Pequots were the dominant tribe in eastern Connecticut. My ancestors were in southwest Connecticut. The Pequots were a hated clan that held many local tribes under their power. They forced these tribes to pay for protection. The name "Pequot" means *destroyer*. In the days of my ancestors, many Indians feared the Pequots even more than they feared the White Man.

The Pequots wanted to control the sacred wampum so they could control the trade with the Whites. But the Whites wanted to control the wampum themselves. So they moved to eliminate the Pequots.

Wopigwooit was the Pequot sachem. When he died, there was a struggle for control of the tribe. Two Indians—Sassacus and Uncas—wanted to be the new Pequot leader. Their dispute split the tribe. When Sassacus was chosen chief, Uncas formed his own tribe—the Mohegans—and turned to the English for help.

And the English were glad to help. Uncas was a traitor. He worked with the White Man against his own people.

In 1637, Uncas helped the English massacre the Pequots. The English and their Mohegan allies took the Pequots by surprise, in the middle of the night, asleep at the Pequot fort near the Mystic River. Their wigwams were set afire, and within an hour seven hundred Pequots were murdered. Men, women, and children.

The remaining Pequot warriors, at a second fort, fled westward. They crossed the Pootatuck River into Paugussett territory. They hid at a fort in a swamp in what today is the town of Southport. This fort was a Paugussett fort.

The fort was surrounded. And many Pequots were killed as they tried to escape. Captain Mason, who was in charge of the English troops, brought out some survivors who were sold as slaves in the West Indies to pay for the expenses of the war. Other survivors were dispersed among the various tribes. Uncas, the traitor, saw it done. And the Pequots ceased to exist.

And for aiding the Pequots in their flight, my ancestors suffered the consequences. When time came to establish legal rights to the land, the White Man claimed the Paugussett territory *by conquest*.

But the Paugussett nation did not fight. And for helping their brothers, my ancestors lost their land.

CHAPTER FOUR

PAUGUSSETTS. PEQANNOCKS. PEQUOTS. It sounds like that nursery rhyme: *Peter Piper picked a peck of...*

Peter Piper. Not Aurelius Piper. But do not get the tribes confused. The Pequannocks were one of the five tribes of the Paugussett confederacy. My ancestors came from that tribe. The Paugussetts were another of the five tribes. They gave their name to the entire group. The Pequots were the *destroyers*. The White Man wiped them out. Then my ancestors lost their land.

That is what I want to talk about next. The land.

Before the White Man came, the land was not a problem. There was plenty of land for all the tribes. Half a million acres for the Paugussett nation. But in the years following the massacre of the Pequots, the English settlements grew rapidly. The settlers pushed westward along the coast of Connecticut. The town of New Haven was settled in 1638, then Milford and Stratford in 1639. By the year 1642, there were new towns along the coast—Fairfield, Norwalk, Stamford, and Greenwich.

Relations between the Indians and the English were poor. The settlers feared that the Connecticut tribes would join together to make war against them. That is what the Indians along the Hudson River did—they joined together to make war against the Dutch in New York. But there is no evidence that my ancestors ever planned to fight the colonists.

My ancestors had to pay wampum to the White Man for his protection. If they failed to pay, the White Man caused them problems. The White Man was disturbing the patterns of the wild game, making it difficult for my ancestors to hunt. His cattle and sheep and pigs roamed everywhere, trampling the Indian cornfields.

And the actions of the Indians were misunderstood. In 1645 the Wepawaugs, one of the five Paugussett tribes, set fire to the woods near Milford. This was a common practice, to clear the underbrush for better hunting. But the White settlers thought the Wepawaugs were making war.

And while my ancestors were struggling to live beside the White Man, the Whites fought among themselves over who owned the land. The Indians had no say. Their land had been *conquered*. My ancestors didn't understand about owning the land. The land is forever. Man merely walks upon the land, then is gone.

In agreeing to sell the land, the Indians thought that they were only agreeing to let the White Man *use* the land. But the Whites talked of *owning* the land. They wanted to buy it. They made deals that the Indians didn't understand. They bought the entire center of the town of Milford for one kettle, six coats, ten blankets, twelve hatchets, twelve hoes, twenty-four knives, and twelve small hand mirrors.

In such a manner the Indian land was lost.

Finally, in 1658, the settlers of Stratford and Fairfield had a border dispute over where to draw the line between the two towns. My ancestors of the Pequannock tribe were caught right in the middle. They were living within their *cleared field*, halfway between Stratford and Fairfield in what today is the city of Bridgeport. So the settlers decided to take over the Pequannock territory and put the tribe on a reservation, eighty acres of land at a place called Golden Hill.

In Bridgeport today there is a street called Golden Hill. My ancestors became known as the Golden Hill Tribe. The name came from certain characteristics of those eighty acres—either the yellow mica in the soil or the sun shining on the tassels of corn.

That is where my ancestors had to live. Those eighty acres formed one of the first Indian reservations in America. The reservation was set up in 1659 to get my ancestors out of the way of the citizens of Stratford and Fairfield.

It was supposed to be a permanent home, as long as the Indians didn't abandon it. But the Whites burned them out and ran them off the land.

CHAPTER FIVE

ON THE BACK BEDROOM WALL of my log home hangs my *gustoweha*, the sacred headdress of my tribe. It is entrusted to my care because I am Chief Big Eagle. Every part of the headdress is special. Every part is a symbol that tells a story.

The U-shaped frame of the gustoweha is made of ash. Ash is a strong but elastic wood that is plentiful in Connecticut. It is used to make canoes, bows, arrows, spears, bowls, spoons, and wigwam poles. The ash frame reminds us of our Brother-the-Tree.

The deer horns of the gustoweha represent the chieftainship. They signify the leader, the sachem. The deer is a noble animal.

The turkey feathers of the gustoweha are long, thin, and brown. They remind us of those that feed us, of the plump birds that once clucked in every thicket.

The red plume reminds us of the scalps of our enemies. Scalps of both White men and Indians. Scalps that ran red when taken. But in the early days of my ancestors there was no scalping. Scalping was a practice introduced by the Europeans.

The fur on the gustoweha reminds us of *mah'ing 'an*, the great animal. Our Brother-the-Wolf. The wolf roamed the forests before the White Man came, before the White Man brought him, like the Indians, to the brink of extinction. Let me talk a minute about the wolves:

In the days of my ancestors, there were many similarities between the wolves and Indians. The wolves and the Indians came and went in the night. They stared at the White Man from the edge of his fields. They made the White Man uneasy. They threatened his livestock. They had powerful hearing. An Indian could put his ear to the ground and hear you approaching. A wolf could hear a cow chewing its cud. Wolves ate grass to scour their intestines. Indians ate herbs. Both marked out their hunting territory. Both were loyal to family. In scarce times, the hunters ate first. In bad times, they fought among themselves. And both Indians and wolves had their own sign language.

Indians have great respect for mah'ing 'an.

There is also wampum on my headdress. Colorful strings of sacred beads. In time, beads joined the quahog shells on the belts of wampum. Wampum was a source of power and pride. But when the White Man came, it became an object of greed.

The deer hooves on my gustoweha remind us of clothing, tools, and food—all the things that our bountiful Brother-the-Deer provided. Like corn, the deer was essential to life.

And finally, the red fox tail reminds us of Uncas. Uncas the Fox, *the one who circles*. The name is appropriate, because Uncas was crafty and cunning. It was Uncas who formed the Mohegan tribe when Sassacus became chief of the Pequots. It was Uncas who saw the Pequots destroyed.

In 1826 a man named James Fenimore Cooper wrote a book called *The Last of the Mohicans*. In this book he called Uncas a *noble savage* and *a friend to Whites*. It is unfortunate for the truth of history that such a book was written because Uncas was a deceitful trickster who played both Whites and Indians against each other.

After the massacre of the Pequots, Uncas gave up all claims to the Pequot land. He said that the land was now the rightful property of the Connecticut Colony. And with the Pequot land went the land of my ancestors.

Do not forget this Uncas. I will speak of him again. He was a fat and drunken traitor who eventually was hated by all—Whites and Indians alike. The gustoweha tells his story too.

The gustoweha tells the story of my ancestors, of their way of life, my heritage. Like my people, it deserves a permanent home.

CHAPTER SIX

AFTER THE GOLDEN HILL RESERVATION was set up for my ancestors, conditions grew worse for the Indians in Connecticut. Relations with the White Man were bad. Finally, several tribes did join together, as the colonists had feared, in an attempt to rid themselves of the White Man's rule.

The five tribes of the Paugussett nation did not take part. But farther to the east, the warriors of Wampanoag went on the warpath with the Narragansett tribe. They were led by Metacom, who was called King Philip by the English. White historians speak of this as King Philip's War, this last-ditch attempt at self-respect.

The fighting lasted from 1675 to 1676, and it ended badly for the Indians. They were soundly defeated in a battle at Mystic, just like the Pequots had been. After that massacre, the White Man's rule was never again challenged.

And once again, Uncas the Fox played a role. He was old now, fat, and always drunk. He did whatever he could to aid the Whites, while seeking favorable treatment for himself and the Mohegans. Years earlier, Uncas had captured Miantonomow, sachem of the Narragansetts, and saw him murdered. Now he helped the English destroy the Narragansett tribe, just as he had helped them destroy the Pequots.

Uncas lived to be nearly one hundred years old. He died in disgrace in 1683. Do not forget him. I will speak of him yet again. Remember this Uncas and King Philip's War.

After this war, much of the Indian land in Connecticut was lost by sale, outright theft, or encroachment. Encroachment is an evil, creeping form of trespassing in which all rights of Indians are disregarded. It was a sad time. There was no longer enough land for the traditional practices. Indian territories stood surrounded by White settlements. And for the first time in ten thousand years of Native American history, my ancestors were forced to adapt to the ways of the White Man in order to survive.

Many of the Paugussett people chose to move instead. They migrated westward beyond their original tribal lands. Others went north. But some remained. In 1680 there were nearly one hundred wigwams on Golden Hill. And in that year the Paugussetts complained to the General Court of the Connecticut Colony in Hartford over the loss of reservation land. The eighty acres were diminishing steadily, due to White encroachment and illegal sales.

An investigation was held, and the tribe was awarded one hundred acres at a place called Coram Hill on the west bank of the Housatonic River. This was the second site of the Paugussett reservation. Today, Old Coram Road is not far from the River Road in Shelton.

But only a few of my ancestors chose to move to Coram Hill. The soil there was poor. The rocky land made farming difficult. The tribe had also been awarded fishing and hunting rights, but the wild game was disappearing. The forests were disappearing too.

By 1710 only twenty-five wigwams sat on Golden Hill. In 1714 twenty acres at Corum Hill were sold. Another plot was sold ten years later. The tribe needed the money in order to live. More and more sales depleted the reservation until the Paugussett nation was forced to break up.

Then many tribal members pushed farther west into New York to join the Iroquois and other tribes of the Oneida nation. The Oneidas offered help and shelter, and most of the Paugussetts went there. Others went north to what is known as Schaghticoke or New Milford. Some went to Stockbridge, Massachusetts. And some went as far west as the Wisconsin territory, where they can still be found today.

Those that remained in the Bridgeport area had to accustom themselves to the White Man. They had to attend his schools. They had to accept his Christian god.

By 1760 only six acres were left out of the original eighty acres at

Golden Hill. The neighbors constantly antagonized my ancestors. They burned down their wigwams and forced them to leave. And it was easier to go than to endure such humiliation because the local officials ignored all complaints.

But the smoke from those burning wigwams rose into the sky. It reached the Creator. Smoke always reaches the Creator. That is why we offer tobacco and sweet grass to the ceremonial fires. Because the Creator sees the sacred smoke.

I want you to remember this—that the smoke of those burning wigwams reached the Creator. Remember the smoke and Uncas and King Philip's War. I will speak of them all again.

CHAPTER SEVEN

ON THE BASEMENT WALL of my log house hangs a prayer that I like to say from time to time. It gives me strength. It helps me be patient in telling my story. Here is that prayer:

Believe that you are a child of the Creator, that you were born pure, with a goodness and strength that all His children are born with. Believe that, if you have strayed from the teachings of your Elders, you are not lost. Readjust your ways and the Creator will give you the vision and power to believe in yourself. Acknowledge the Creator, through Thanksgiving and prayer, for the strength to do what is right. Ask the Elders for counseling to guide your life back to the wisdom of our old ways. Be not discouraged. Make your life calm and rewarding. Find peace and acquire serenity. Believe that with the Creator's help, you can regain control.

The Creator has a purpose for everything. He created the Native People in his image and gave them Natural Law to follow. We are relatives to all living things on Mother Earth. We are thankful for each day that is given to us by the Creator. He gave us a sacred pipe, tobacco and sweet grass, and ceremonies to cleanse our souls. We have sweat lodges to purify our bodies. We were given a mind and soul to look after all His creations— the plants, animals, and winged creatures, as well as this wonderful land. The Creator's Law of Nature is supreme. We must offer our children a life of hope and the right to live as instructed by the Creator. We must listen to our Elders and heed the Creator's will.

Unfortunately, the White Man has always lived by his own rules. He has his own way of doing things. He made life miserable for my ancestors. By the end of the eighteenth century, only one family lived on the Golden Hill reservation—the family of Tom Sherman. Tom Sherman was the last chief to live on the original reservation land. What is left of the Paugussett people today comes from that Sherman family at Golden Hill.

There were seven members of the family, and there were only six acres of land among them. And before long those six acres were threatened too.

So the Shermans petitioned the General Court in Hartford, and there was an investigation into their complaints. Once again, the Court decided in favor of the Indians. The Shermans were awarded nineteen and three-quarter acres of land at a place called Turkey Meadows here in Trumbull. Today, Turkey Meadows Road is just to the north of here by several blocks. That was the third site of the Paugussett reservation.

By 1800 the land that remained to the tribe at Corum Hill was gone. The tribal members were always in debt. So the land at Corum Hill was sold by Indian agents, and the money was put into the bank. The tribe was supposed to live off the interest. But you can read in the State of Connecticut records *that the agents merely ate up the profits before the Indians ever got a penny.* And yet it had been made clear that *the interest would be granted to the individuals until they became extinct.*

In 1842 the interest alone came to $1175. That was a lot of money in those days. But the Indians never saw it. Their money disappeared just like their land. My ancestors were supposed to receive payment two times a year *until they became extinct.* Why couldn't they have used the word *forever?* You don't use the word *extinct* unless you have something in mind.

In the following years, in the same way, the nineteen and three-quarter acres at Turkey Meadows were sold, stolen, or deeded away by Indian agents. But in 1875, the Sherman family bought back a quarter-acre of that land from Charles Ambler. It was signed over to Russell Tomlinson, an Indian agent, to be held for the Golden Hill tribe. When Tomlinson died, my great-grandfather William Sherman signed the quarter-acre over to another agent, Roland Lacy.

And when Lacy died in 1886, the state of Connecticut

became the trustee of the land and set it aside as a permanent reservation site.

This was the fourth site of the Golden Hill reservation. It is the quarter-acre on which my log house sits today.

Had I been born three hundred years earlier, I would have walked freely with my Paugussett brothers on half a million acres of land. Through the centuries that half a million acres has shrunk to almost nothing. A quarter-acre is less than half the size of a football field. It is all there is left of one of the oldest Indian reservations in America.

It is not very much room for an Indian nation.

CHAPTER EIGHT

I HAVE SPOKEN of the Creator. But the first White men to come to America called the Indians *pagan* and *heathen* because the Indians didn't worship the White Man's god.

The Indians worshiped the sun. We still do. We pray to the east, where the sun rises. We thank the sun for each day, for its heat and light.

The White Man worships the sun too, but he doesn't realize it. He puts thousands of dollars of glass panels on his roof to capture the sun's rays. For solar energy. So why should the *Indian* be called *pagan?*

In the back yard of our quarter-acre reservation is a sweat lodge. It is a small, dome-shaped wigwam covered with mats and bark. There is a fire pit inside. Large, smooth stones are placed in the center, in each of the four directions—north, south, east, west. And there is a large stone in the middle, signifying the center of the earth.

The rocks are heated. Then the medicine man pours water on them, making steam. The Indians kneel around the rocks and sweat. After the ceremony is over, they jump into the creek.

The sweat lodge is for ceremonial purification. It is a cleansing. Like the White Man's baptism. Really, the religious beliefs of the White Man and the Indians are not so very far apart. We must work together to see the similarities, not the differences.

But sometimes I find it hard to understand the White Man. Look at the new housing developments around here. The first thing the developer does is cut down all the trees. Then the people complain that their grass won't grow. It burns up in summer. Trees give off hundreds of gallons of water in summer. But they can't help you if you cut them down.

And the White Man hates weeds. Especially dandelions. The first thing the White Man does when he tries to grow a lawn is to get rid of all the dandelions. As soon as he sees a dandelion, he kills it. But the Indian *eats* it.

In the spring, the dandelions are tender. Tender dandelions are good to eat. They are full of iron. They are excellent for cleansing the system, for cleansing the blood. But the White Man kills them in his own back yard. Then he goes to the health food store and buys dandelions for his salad.

The White Man and the Indians must share their ideas for a better understanding.

But one thing the White Man doesn't seem to understand is that the land is necessary to survive. Without the land there is no survival. You *can* survive on the land if you treat it right. You can't if you grab it and develop it.

Indians have an old saying:

I wonder if the ground has anything to say? I wonder if the ground is listening to what is said? I wonder if the ground would come alive to what is on it?

The earth has much to say, but no one listens. And yet the Earth Mother is all we have.

CHAPTER NINE

AN ITALIAN CAN GO BACK TO ITALY. A Greek can go back to Greece. But where can an Indian go? He has no place to go.

There are more than one hundred members of the Golden Hill tribe. For the past century we have had but a quarter-acre of this earth to ourselves, a quarter-acre remnant of one of the oldest, continuous Indian reservations in America. It is something you never read about in history books. Because the history books are written by White men. They do not tell the true story of what happened to the Indians.

The White Man teaches that Columbus discovered America. So why not teach, too, that the Golden Hill Indian Reservation in Trumbull, Connecticut, is the home of the Paugussett Nation? That it was one of the very first Indian reservations in America? That it is still here? That it will always be here?

I was raised on this quarter-acre. I will die here. It is my home and the home of my ancestors.

But in 1976, a White neighbor tried to drive me off this quarter-acre and claim it for himself. He claimed that he had bought this land years ago when he bought the property next door. America was two hundred years old in 1976. It was the year of the Bicentennial. And within a few days of America's two hundredth birthday—within a few days of the Fourth of July, 1976—a White American tried to run me off this land. Just as his ancestors had run off my ancestors for hundreds of years.

Nothing changes. Americans do not learn very easily.

Years ago, my grandfather told me that one day someone would try to take this land; that people would say we didn't own this land. I didn't believe him. But he was right. I believe him now.

But there was another celebration in 1976. A *Tri*centennial. It was the three hundredth anniversary of King Philip's War. The Indians' last attempt to get rid of White rule in Connecticut. That last-ditch attempt at self-respect. The coincidence of those dates is ironic. While White Americans were celebrating a Bicentennial, the Paugussetts were celebrating a Tricentennial.

Then we went to war over this quarter-acre.

The descendants of Uncas the Fox played a role too. I will get to that later. I will tell you about that war in due time. But to understand it, you must first know some other things.

The log house in which I now live with my family was completed in June of 1977. It took more than a year and a half to build. That is a long time to build such a small house. The state of Connecticut built it for me. It took a long time because of the war for this quarter-acre.

But for more than one hundred years there was another house on this land. The homestead of the Sherman family. I was born in Bridgeport in 1916 and brought to the Sherman homestead on this quarter-acre. It was already an old house, even then. I lived there until my mother moved us to Bridgeport to go to school.

The Sherman homestead was built in 1875. It was a two-story frame house with vertical planking on the outside. Through the years it became quite shabby. It was covered with tarpaper. Then clapboards. Finally aluminum siding. The roof leaked. A large chimney ran up through several rooms. Before this old house was torn down, that chimney was walking. The bricks were shifting. You could see the flames right through the cracks.

The house was old and in need of repair. There was an outhouse out back. There had been no bathroom until the Shermans had one put in, with a septic system, in 1963. It was an old place, but it was my childhood home.

And when the time came to tear down that old house, a bulldozer started at the right front corner and dropped it right on its foundation. Within an hour, the old house was laid flat.

I felt sad because it was the home of my ancestors. I felt happy because the new log house would belong to the tribe. Because the quarter-acre would be ours forever.

CHAPTER TEN

MY FATHER WAS A CHEROKEE from South Carolina. My mother was Ethel Sherman, Pequannock blood. My uncle was Ed Sherman, Chief Black Hawk. Our family tree goes back thirty generations.

And yet, when the war for this quarter-acre began in 1976, I had to prove that I was an Indian. My neighbor claimed that this land was his, and he claimed that I wasn't an Indian, that I had no right to live on this land. I had to prove who I was. My papers are on file in Hartford. I'm an Indian, all right. I was raised right here on this quarter-acre.

It was not easy growing up as an Indian. I attended elementary school in Nichols. Then, when I was in the fourth grade, my mother moved to Bridgeport to give my sister and me a better education in the city. We lived on Newfield Avenue, then Olive Street, Lindley Street, North Washington Avenue, and Iranistan Avenue. The last school I attended in Bridgeport was St. Augustine's.

And I can still hear the words of my grandfather: *You take those kids to the city and you will catch more hell than you'll ever catch in your entire life*. And he was right. He knew what he was talking about. Just like when he said that one day people would claim this land for their own.

None of the kids would play with us. They said we were odd. My sister had long hair. The teachers used to put their fingers in her hair to get a grip, then slap her back and forth across the face. I got into trouble, fighting to protect her.

We were always hungry. I worked the carnivals—Ringling Brothers, Barnum & Bailey, and others. I worked as a rigger and a roustabout, and I did the Western shows. And then I ran away. I was nine years old.

The first time I left home I went to the Samp Mortar Reservoir in Easton and stayed a week to ten days. I left at night and traveled by night. In those days most of the children who had the room, and the woodlots, used packing crates for clubhouses. That's what I looked for and that's what I stayed in during the day time. The kids would bring me food and cigarettes.

Later, I went to Massachusetts and New Hampshire. In northern New Hampshire the paved road became a gravel road, then a dirt road, and at the end of the dirt road was a farmhouse. I stopped at the farm and worked for the farmer, helping him with the hay. The man sensed what I was doing and said I had to get rid of my knickers. So he bought me my first pair of long pants. And he made me two pairs of boots, the kind that buckled with a button hook.

I stayed on that farm the first winter, then in the spring I took to the woods, following a logging trail until it went out of existence and there was nothing but Mother Nature and me—no one to make fun of me or to treat me like dirt. I was free.

I lived in the woods for three years, surviving the winters. I lived like my ancestors. And one day I wound up in Westfield, Maine, with a family by the name of Gordon Tweedy. The Tweedys were potato farmers. They said I was the only wild Indian that ever came naked out of those woods. They had to chase me to catch me.

So I was raised in the backwoods of Maine. I learned to hunt, fish, and trap; to be a logger, a woodsman, and a farmer. My foster parents were Gordon Tweedy and his wife, and they took care of me until my mother came to get me and take me home.

In 1970 my former wife and I made a trip to Maine. She could not believe that I had survived in those woods as a boy. And when she met the people there, they told her that my bed was still waiting, just like it was when I left.

But my mother brought me home from Maine. And at the age of fifteen I went to work in a steel mill, at the Stanley Works, loading steel. But before long I was on the road again. I hopped freight trains all over this country. And then I went into the Navy.

I fought for this country in World War II. On November 8, 1942, at 5:00 a.m., I took part in the invasion of North Africa. I was aboard the *U.S.S. Thomas Jefferson*, an attack transport. We landed in French Morocco, the first wave to hit the beachhead.

Life in the Navy was hell. At that time there were only White southerners in the Navy, and even in war time they couldn't understand why I was up on the top deck, a seaman before the captain's mast, not down in the kitchen with the Blacks. The Blacks slept in a little iron cell off the mess hall and had to wait on the others. Any minority that was not White got the same treatment. You lived and slept with the fear of being thrown overboard. But when the general alarm sounded, and I was in the five-inch gun crew on the bow, there was no question of race or color. It was load and fire, and they forgot I was an Indian.

Many people don't realize how American Indians helped to win World War II. The Japanese had broken our code, so we used Navajo talkers on the air waves. But I wanted out of the Navy because of the prejudice. So I was mustered out—right into the Army!

After the war, in 1945, I went to work for a trucking company, National Transportation Freight Lines, in Bridgeport. But I was never treated like the other drivers. So I bought myself a truck and went into business for myself.

People think that because you own your own trucks and run cross country, you've got a great life. But there is a lonesomeness in it. It's hard on your wife when you are out on the road, working hard just to pay the bills on those trucks, let alone earning money to send home. It's a hard life, not a great life.

When I retired in 1969, I had seven trucks. I was made to retire because of a heart attack. I was not allowed to drive any more. So I went back to Maine because the people of Maine have a good thing. They don't allow their country to be torn up.

I retired to Maine and went back to the mountains. Because in the mountains you can be free.

CHAPTER ELEVEN

I RETURNED TO THIS QUARTER-ACRE in the summer of 1973. I came back because Chief Black Hawk, my uncle Ed Sherman, asked me to. He was eighty-four years old and dying of cancer. He was living in the old Sherman homestead with his wife Evelyn, who was seventy-two and crippled with arthritis.

The house was a mess. Tarpaper blowing off the roof. My uncle had had a bathroom put in. The Indian agent told him to go ahead and have a bathroom put in, to send the bill to the state. So he did. But the state wouldn't pay the bill. My uncle had cancer and was too old to fight. So I came home to this quarter-acre, to make it a decent place for an old man to die.

My uncle Ed Sherman once performed with the Wild West show of Annie Oakley and Buffalo Bill Cody. He would get all dressed up in his full regalia—gustoweha, fringed jacket and pants, beads, bracelets. He had his picture in the newspaper.

But Indians don't go around dressed up like that. It would be stupid. You couldn't go hunting. My Uncle Ed did it because it was what the White Man wanted to see. It was what the White Man thought an Indian was like. Ed Sherman was a mechanic for the White Line Bus Company. That name is very ironic. Because Indians have always had to toe the White Man's line.

The White Man giveth and the White Man taketh. That is what my Uncle Ed always said. He died in February of 1974, before the war for this quarter-acre started. It was good that he died then. He was used to more tranquil ways. He wanted to live at the old homestead and die in peace.

I respected that. There was no abuse from the neighbors while

I was here with him. He could have been sent to a convalescent home, but the state would not have paid the bill. So the doctor sent him home to die. He was eighty-four years old. He had cancer of the rectum. He bled for three days. When he started to bleed, we took him to the hospital. Then his heart gave out.

The Indian Affairs Coordinator from the state of Connecticut came to the hospital. He wanted to OK the transfer of tribal authority from Chief Black Hawk to myself. Mainly he was there because the doctor was worried about getting his money from the state.

The state Welfare Department was in charge of Indian Affairs until just a few months before Ed Sherman died. And the state law that applied, under *Aliens and Indians*, 1961, section 4765, says: *The Welfare Commission shall have the care and management of lands and buildings on reservations . . . and of all people residing on such reservations and shall provide assistance to needy Indians on reservations in an amount necessary to maintain a standard of living reasonably compatible with health and decency.*

But the state wouldn't pay for the bathroom that Ed Sherman had had put in. The Indian agent had told him to go ahead and get one put in, then the state said he didn't have permission. And then they kept his insurance money. I fought them, but I couldn't get it back.

They sent me a letter: *Reimbursement of welfare payments is required from the assets of welfare recipients, and there are no exceptions.* When I asked about the tribal funds, the money from the sale of Indian land that should have been accumulating interest all these years, I was told: *To our knowledge there is no tribal fund for the Golden Hill Indians.*

The state was supposed to take care of Ed Sherman. Instead, they took his insurance money. That was a breach of their own trust as established by law.

I had to get permission from the Indian Affairs Coordinator to come home to this reservation to help Ed Sherman die. I had to get permission to bring my wife and son on this reservation after Ed Sherman passed away. It is a sad thing when you have to get permission to go into your own home. Even to *visit* a reservation, an Indian needs permission.

The last thing Ed Sherman said to me was: *You are now Chief.*

Take over now and give 'em all the hell they can stand. And when the war for this quarter-acre began, that is exactly what I did.

My aunt, Evelyn Sherman, died a few months after my uncle, in the spring of 1974. She was seventy-two. She just told me one morning that she was going to die. She said she had lived like a queen while I was there, that I had treated her like a queen. She felt a heart attack coming on. And the heart attack came just like she said it would.

Then I got permission to bring my wife and son to this quarter-acre. My son Kenny, whose Indian name is Moon Face, was just a young teenager then. In many ways he was a typical teenager, with a mind of his own. Everything I told him not to do, he did.

One day, when I had to go away to a meeting in Hartford, I told him: *Kenny, don't even strike a match while I'm gone.* And when I got back, he had a big bonfire going. The fire department was here, and the police, and the forest rangers, and the bonfire was going up into the pine trees. I said: *Kenny, didn't I tell you not to have a fire?* And he said: *It's my land too. I can do what I please.*

Teenagers have a lot to learn. And Kenny learned more than he wanted to know during the war for this quarter-acre. He learned what it means to be an Indian. I'm glad he's proud of the land.

After the Shermans died, I set to work to get the old homestead fixed up. By law, the state of Connecticut had to do it. I want to explain about that.

Until 1973 no one in the state would admit to being an Indian. There were more than twenty-two hundred Indians living in Connecticut, according to the 1970 census, but no one would admit to being an Indian. Then all that changed. It actually began in the late 1960s, when everybody was *doing their own thing.* The Black people said, *Black is beautiful.* They found Black power. And the Indians found power too. A national organization called AIM—the American Indian Movement—helped Indians take pride in themselves and their past.

Until then, the Indians had lived under the White Man's thumb. Indians in Connecticut were under the thumb of the state Welfare Department, which had controlled Indian affairs in Connecticut since 1941. They believed that the Indians couldn't handle their own business. They felt that the Indians would be better off living like White men. So the state discouraged the use of reservations. If you wanted to live on a reservation, you had to deal with uncooperative officials. Indians were being denied the right to live and gather as a tribe.

The rules were unfair. To live on a reservation, you had to apply in writing. You couldn't build any buildings without permission. And if you got permission, you could only build on approved sites. Or the building would be removed. You needed permission to make repairs and improvements. An Indian agent told my Uncle Ed to go ahead and put in a bathroom. That seemed permission enough. But the state wouldn't pay the bill. And you couldn't do any business on the reservation because the reservation could not control any funds.

The Welfare Department decided who was an Indian and who was not, who could live on the reservation and who couldn't. You couldn't tell them anything because they didn't care. And they couldn't tell *you* anything because they didn't know anything. Every time you'd write, the answer would come back that so-and-so *isn't handling Indian Affairs any more*. There were only seven Indians receiving welfare payments in the entire state of Connecticut, so the Welfare Department should never have been in charge of Indian Affairs.

The Welfare Department was an enemy to the Indians through its indifference. It was hampering the Indians' efforts to gain control of their own destiny. But all that changed in 1973 with the passage of Public Act 73-660. That law created an Indian Affairs Division and put it under the jurisdiction of the state's Environmental Protection Department. It created the Connecticut Indian Affairs Council as well, with representatives from all the state tribes.

But when the Council was being formed, the Golden Hill tribe was not included. Only Ed Sherman and his wife were on the reservation then. Just two old people, one dying of cancer and the other crippled with arthritis. Many people felt they were the only remaining Indians of the Paugussett Nation.

They received a phone call, but they didn't want to be bothered. They didn't understand what was happening in Hartford. And they didn't care, because they were dying. So the Golden Hill tribe was not included in the plans for the Council. Tribal members were scattered throughout the state and throughout the nation. Because they had no tribal land. Just a quarter-acre lot of scrub brush and pine.

Just one old house and two old people.

CHAPTER TWELVE

PUBLIC ACT 73-660, which went into effect on October 1, 1973, gave the Indians of Connecticut full rights as citizens. It provided care and management and maintenance of reservations. It granted hunting, fishing, and trapping rights. It determined the qualifications of an Indian. And it created the Connecticut Indian Affairs Council.

It was not an easy law to get passed. The Governor gave no support. So the Indians around the state got together to learn the ways of the lawmakers. The first bill they presented to the legislature would have given the Indians of Connecticut complete control over their own affairs. That bill got nowhere. Public Act 73-660 was a compromise bill. The Indians only got partial control. But it was a start.

The Connecticut Indian Affairs Council was created to give the Indians a voice. The tribes that formed the Council were the Eastern Pequots, the Western Pequots, the Schaghticokes, and the Mohegans. The Paugussetts, as I said, were not included. I sat in on the Council meetings as a non-voting member for one year, until the Golden Hill tribe was added to the CIAC by special legislation in 1974.

They actually did me a favor. I had to prove who I was, who my ancestors were. They put my papers on file. So when the war for this quarter-acre began two years later, and my neighbors claimed that I wasn't an Indian, the proof was already on file in Hartford.

But I believe that if you are going to tell the true story, then you leave nothing out. The Indians themselves had excluded the Paugussetts from the Connecticut Indian Affairs Council. This amounted to termination of the tribe. And the Mohegans were put in *as a courtesy*. The Mohegans were included even though they have no reservation today. They have no reservation because Uncas the Fox gave away their land to his White friends years ago.

In the 1800s, when the Mohegans petitioned for the right to be citizens, their tribal members accepted individual plots of land, no common tribal ground. So the Mohegans today have no reservation. They were not supposed to be on the bill that formed the Council. But they were. And the Paugussetts, who have one of the oldest reservations in America, were left out.

At a meeting on the Eastern Pequot reservation, one of the Mohegan Indians stated that he was called before the legislature and a compromise was made—that the Golden Hill tribe would be no more, and the Department of Environmental Protection could keep the Golden Hill tribal funds. The original funds are still being researched by Indian lawyers.

I have that meeting on tape. And when I asked this Mohegan, would he sell an Indian tribe down the river, he answered: *It's a foot in the door. Half a loaf is better than none.* A foot in the White Man's door. Then he said that the legislature had said it and done it, not him.

And so you see once, once again, that a Mohegan was trying to do away with another tribe, while seeking favor for himself, just like Uncas the Fox helped destroy the Indian tribes years ago.

So I called Irving Harris, Chief of the Schaghticokes, who was in charge of creating the Council. And I told him to meet me at the Merritt Parkway entrance in Stratford, because I was going to take my tape to the Governor to find out the truth. Because this Mohegan had said that his tribe hadn't made the proposal, the Governor had.

On hearing the tape played, Irving Harris threw his arms about wildly and raised hell. He said, *No, the Governor hadn't done it. The Indians themselves had wiped out the Golden Hill tribe. Because when they telephoned, there were just two old people on the Golden Hill reservation, who didn't want to be bothered.*

This Mohegan wanted to blame the Welfare Department too, for *obstructing the efforts* at determining the true membership of the Golden Hill tribe. But in the end it was easier to sell a tribe down the river.

In the seventeenth century, the Indians of Connecticut were fighting among themselves to gain the favor of the White Man. Three hundred and fifty years later, the problem continues. And the descendants of Uncas the Fox are still at work.

CHAPTER THIRTEEN

I HAVE SAID that Public Act 73-660 determined the qualifications for an Indian. To qualify as an Indian in Connecticut today, you have to have one-eighth blood of a Connecticut tribe, participate in tribal activities, and be recognized as an Indian by other Indians. That is what makes you an Indian. It is an improvement over the old way.

The old way was that the White Man decided who was an Indian. There was an official *blood quota*. You had to have a certain amount of Indian blood to be an Indian. But the percentage would change—one-half, one-quarter, one-eighth—according to the needs of the politicians. If it was to their benefit to have a lot of Indians on the state rolls, the amount of Indian blood was low, so you had a lot of Indians. If they wanted few Indians, the percentage was high.

In the south today some states consider you Black if your percentage of Black blood is only one thirty-second. But how Black does that make you? Almost White.

The blood quota was being used to make the eastern Indians extinct. At one point, to be an Indian, you had to marry within your own tribe. But more than half the Paugussetts are from the same family. That means incest. The blood quota was a form of genocide. Public Act 73-660 put an end to that.

It was a good law. It was a start. But there are still many problems. Lack of money is the biggest one. Another is that the Connecticut Indian Affairs Council is not autonomous. It doesn't have complete control over Indian affairs. It is only an advisory voice, a department under a larger agency. What we are working for now is our own agency. An agency just for Indians. With power for Indians.

Public Act 73-660 said that the state of Connecticut must provide for the maintenance of Indian reservations. So I asked the state to fix up the old Sherman homestead. But in the summer of 1974, after the Shermans had died and I was living on this quarter-acre with my wife and son, the state said that it would cost more to fix up that old house than to build a new one.

The state then began what it called the *relocation process.* They offered to move me to another house. They offered to move me to a split-ranch house that the Department of Transportation had acquired in this area. What does an Indian want with a split-ranch house. It is not a traditional house. A log house is a traditional house.

I refused to relocate. The reason was this. I would get a new house, but it would not be on tribal land. Therefore other Indians couldn't live there. Just my family. The tribe would have no home. Relocation would have meant the end of the Golden Hill Reservation and the official termination of the tribe. Because there is an old state law that says you have to live on the reservation for two months of the year to be considered a full-time resident. Otherwise, the land ceases to be a reservation. I was not going to take that chance.

Had I moved, the state would have put up a historical marker on the quarter-acre. It would have said something like this: *This is the former site of the Golden Hill Indian Reservation, one of the oldest, continuous reservations in Connecticut; the former home of the Paugussett Indians, the only tribe with a tradition of hereditary one-chief rule.* The state would not have been able to sell this land, because the state—by law—cannot sell Indian land. But the reservation would have been terminated.

So I told the state no. I would not relocate. I would not sell my ancestors down the river for a historical marker.

CHAPTER FOURTEEN

BUT YOU ARE WAITING to hear about the war for this quarter-acre. I am coming to that. What I have been telling you happened before the war. It is nothing compared to the war itself, but it will help you to understand the war. To understand why I have worn a gun. Why blood was shed on this reservation. But first I want to play you a tape recording.

I made this tape in 1975, during the first week in March. I was in the intensive care unit of a local hospital. I had had a heart attack. I had been made to retire from my trucking business because of heart problems. And in March of 1975 I had a heart attack.

I had been working too hard. No sleep. The Indian affairs kept me aggravated. And very angry. The doctor told me to rest, but I couldn't rest. So I had a heart attack. There was a fluttering in my chest. Then a pain. My arm hurt. It was hard to breathe. Then I found myself in an oxygen tent at the hospital. In intensive care. I thought I was going to die. So I made this tape, because I felt the state was going to evict me, to relocate me, and put an end to the reservation forever.

The tape is addressed to the Governor of Connecticut, to the Indian Affairs Coordinator, to the members of the Indian Affairs Council, and to all Indians in Connecticut and America. Here are the words of that tape recording:

We have had a treaty with the United States and the state of Connecticut for over three hundred years, during which they have enjoyed taking the land that is now the city of Bridgeport. Land bought with tribal money in the town of Trumbull has been sold and resold until one quarter-acre remains. The present reservation was bought with Indian money. The land was bought by my great-grandfather William Sherman so that the Golden Hill people would have a reservation. In 1886 the state of Connecticut set it aside as a reservation. It lies on the edge of the nineteen-and-three-quarter acre reservation that was to be protected for the Golden Hill People of the Paugussett Nation. It was illegally sold by an Indian agent.

They say developed land cannot be taken back. You cannot regain it. But as of this day I say, all undeveloped land surrounding the Golden Hill Indian Reservation in Turkey Meadows is the property of the Golden Hill Indians and will be protected as such.

The White Man does nothing for the Indian. When you apply for federal funds, the population of American Indians is included in the sum. But when your boards are set up, there are Whites and Blacks and people with Spanish surnames, but where is the Indian?

We have had a treaty with the United States and the state of Connecticut for over three hundred years, but they have not spent any money on the house on the Golden Hill Reservation since the house was built by my great-grandfather William Sherman. And that is the house that many Indians have lived in, with very little done to keep it up. First the Parks Department had it. Then the Welfare Department had it, and now the Department of Environmental Protection has it. Please be advised that the Golden Hill tribe has historic rights to dwell on their reservation. To remove the tribe from the reservation would amount to the unauthorized termination of tribal rights and would be vigorously opposed.

Reservations were established in the state of Connecticut for the benefit of Native Americans. The Golden Hill tribe of the Paugussett Nation was in fact the first tribe afforded a specific reservation. For over three hundred years the state of Connecticut has continued to recognize the tribal rights. The most recent legislation, Public Act 73-660, says that the reservations shall be maintained for the exclusive benefit of the Indians who reside there. Public Act 73-660 in no way gives the state or any of its agencies the right and authority to terminate the rights of any tribe.

The structure of the Golden Hill Reservation has been neglected to the point where it has become uninhabitable after almost ninety years of continued occupancy. The requests for repairs have been repeatedly ignored, and the structure is now beyond the point where such repairs are feasible. Six months ago a request was made for a new building on the reservation, but no answer has been forthcoming.

Since October of 1973 the Indian Affairs Council has met with nothing but opposition and indifference to its requests for programs. Demands for reservation surveys and title searches provided for by Public Act 73-660 have been ignored. Money set aside for title searches has not been released. The requests for maintenance have fallen on deaf ears. This attitude will no longer be tolerated.

Any attempts to remove the Golden Hill tribe and the members now residing on the reservation to another location, and any attempt to demolish without replacing the present structure on the reservation, shall be met and fought with all the legal tools available. We trust that you will comply with the requirements of the law and not undertake any rash action.

The present Golden Hill Reservation was purchased by my great-grandfather in 1875. Since 1886 the land has been held for the tribe by the state of Connecticut. The land is sacred to the Golden Hill tribe. We will not consent to any resolution that will result in the loss of this reservation land. Nor will the tribe consent to the razing of the present structure, nor the temporary relocation of the Indians residing there to other property owned by the state without the guarantee that the state will continue to provide for a permanent residence for the Golden Hill tribe, on tax-exempt land, after my death.

If I live to move from this hospital, I will declare all land on Shelton Road that lies behind the Golden Hill Reservation, to the right and left, all undeveloped land will be declared as Indian land. No trespassing.

There is no reason why the state cannot build a suitable house for the Golden Hill Indians. We are traditional people. We live traditionally. We want a traditional house set apart from all other houses. A house that costs no more than the average house being built today. Namely, a log house. Because that is what we had as traditional people.

We want no hand-outs. But for over three hundred years you have abused our people. You have taken our lands. You have outright stolen them. You have taken our tribal funds and you have spent them.

Check your records. The money from the sale of Indian land was to go to the tribes. So far no one has issued the check. Nobody knows what happened to the interest on the money put in trust for the Indians. I would like to state here and now that the Indian should no longer be at the mercy of the White Man, who sits behind his typewriter and decides who is White and who is Black and who is a mongrel.

We are Indians. We are proud of it. And we will stand for our rights. If the state says it will terminate us, all the Indians of this country will protect the Golden Hill Reservation.

In 1743 we were offered protection and shelter by the tribes of the Oneida nation. That offer still stands. Many of our people went to the Oneidas, but one family remained on the land. The six tribes of the Oneida nation, and the mighty Sioux, and the Indians of AIM have an interest in what happens to the Golden Hill Reservation and the Golden Hill tribe.

We have tried to do it your way, the White Man's way, through peace. But we will not get down on our knees and beg. We will not crawl, because I am declaring all undeveloped land surrounding the Golden Hill Reservation to be Indian land. Any White person who sets foot on the land will be shot.

We are no longer going to sit by and be third-class citizens. If we have to take it to the Indian nations for help, we will. But we hope that you will take the time to realize and to straighten out the problem. Because for hundreds of years you have done nothing for the Golden Hill Indians. But you have taken much. Your great city of Bridgeport lies on Golden Hill land, which was not paid for. In Trumbull, the land has been sold and resold. The same spot.

We do not want to become enemies of the city. We want to work with the city and live peacefully, just as we wanted to live peacefully with the settlers years ago. But it seems that the Great White Chief in Hartford has said that we shall not have a house. That we shall be terminated. But by the Creator, if we must be terminated, then you will have to shoot us down as dogs, because the Golden Hill Reservation will be protected from this day on.

For years the Golden Hill people have never been able to live as a people on reservation land, to carry on their traditions, their language, their culture. You say we are accepted into White society, but when we go for a job or to the hospital you mark us Black. When an Indian child is born, you mark it Black. Because the form says White or Black. That mark holds us through life.

The only person who should have the say as to who is an Indian is the tribal chief. And as long as I am the tribal chief of the Golden Hill Indians of the Paugussett nation, I shall say who is an Indian and who shall live on the reservation.

We are small, but we will build into a powerful nation, a nation you will hear all the way to the halls of Congress. And if we have to call upon our Indian brothers to protect our land, that too can be arranged.

I hope we can sit down at the table and talk and agree to a compromise. All it takes is a decent house on the Golden Hill Reservation, not only for me and my family, but for other tribal members when I die.

We are lucky that we have members of the original Sherman family left. Look up any deed, any record, and you will find that you are on Sherman land. Indian land given by my forebearers. And before I see the Golden Hill reservation terminated, blood will run from that land. Both White and Indian blood. So help me God.

If the White Man is allowed to terminate the Golden Hill Reservation, then he may do the same to each and every tribe, and not comply with the law. If the state of Connecticut terminates one reservation, the other states will follow suit. It is time that all Indians, regardless of whether they are Sioux, Pequot, Paugussett, Schaghticoke, or whatever, stand together to protect the Indian nation that is to be terminated. Because once we are terminated, we are no more. We are at the mercy of the White Man.

Some people know, some people enjoy this White society. They say it is the greatest democracy in the world. But we have a lot to accomplish to claim to be the greatest democracy. They say you must be one-eighth Indian to reside on the reservation. In some places it is one-half. But all that amounts to is genocide. Because nobody can say who is an Indian but another Indian. A White Man tries to make an Indian what he wants him to be. But there is no way that he can change his heart.

They say that the Indians of AIM are just a bunch of hoodlums, a bunch of drunks. But if it were not for AIM, the Indian situation today would not be in the front. People for years and years and years have forgotten that Indians have a right to exist. And if the Golden Hill people must call upon AIM to protect the land, to see that they have a decent dwelling, then so shall it be. Because my time is short, I do not have much time to live, and the day has come for my people to be protected. The land must be protected forever.

So there is only one thing to do, and that is to call a meeting with our brothers of AIM, the tribes of the Oneida nation, and the mighty Sioux. Because we will not be terminated. Chief Geronimo once said that it is better to die fighting than to be a dog on your knees for the rest of your life.

We will not be dogs. We have been dogs for over three hundred years. Today we are still dogs. But we are what we are. We are Indian people and proud to be Indian. According to Public Act 73-660, we have full rights as citizens and residents of the state of Connecticut. But there is discrimination.

If you want to see discrimination, look at your state house. Out of all your representatives, out of all your people, you do not have an Indian. There is no senator or representative that is an Indian. Who do we go to when we have a problem? Who do we talk to? The Indian Affairs Coordinator is a fine man, but he has no power to make tough decisions. We must have an Indian Bureau, an Indian Commission, by Indians and for Indians.

The honorable Governor of the State of Connecticut claims not to want the $7,000 pay raise that the Governor is supposed to get. The Great White Chief says that the money will be turned back to the Governor's fund. But if the Governor is so compassionate for people, why not give that money to the Indian Affairs Council to help the needy on the reservations?

People need to live. To teach their language in the schools. You have your Black culture. You have your Spanish culture. But who teaches Indian culture to Indian children? If you want discrimination, all you have to do is look from the state capitol to the governments of the cities and towns.

I say this with no hatred and malice in my heart. But I believe it is time that the American Indian is recognized as a decent human being with the right to exist and to live traditionally upon his land if he so chooses. I believe the people of this country should know the true situation, which never gets into the newspapers. The only thing that is shown on TV is John Wayne and his Comancheros. But Indians are not like that. You pass them every day on the street, but you do not recognize them because they do not have feathers growing out of their hair. I believe it is time that the state takes a good look at itself before the American Bicentennial, to see that its Native Americans—the very first Americans—have the right to live as American people too.

I thank you.

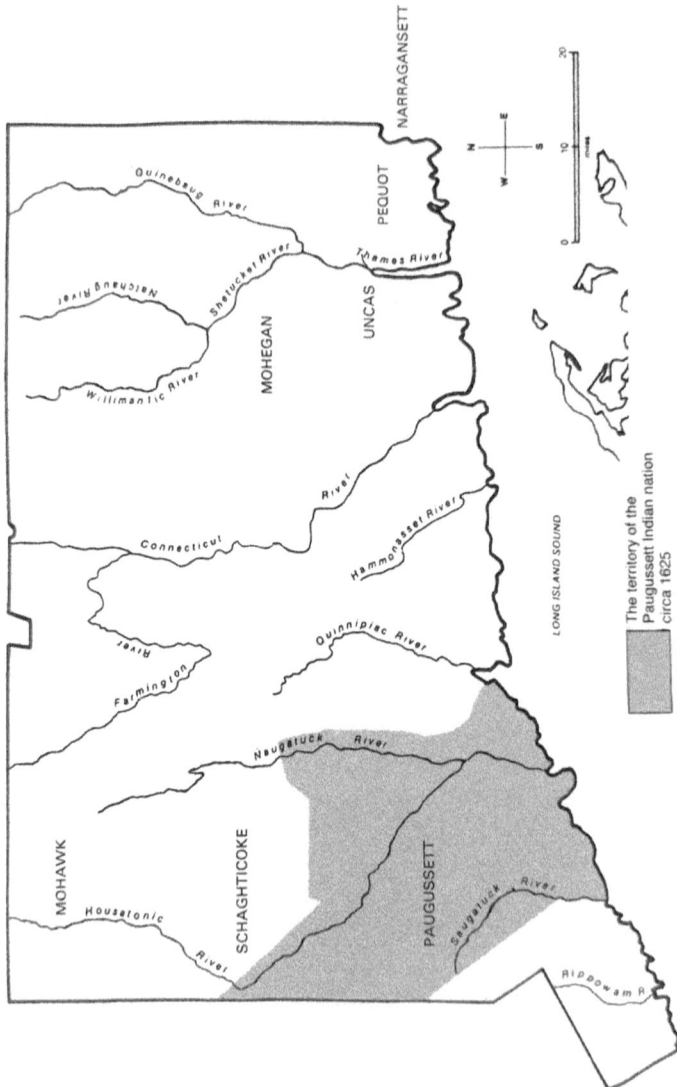

The state of Connecticut, showing the approximate territory of the Golden Hill (Paugussett) Indians circa 1625, and the location of other tribes mentioned by Chief Big Eagle in this book.

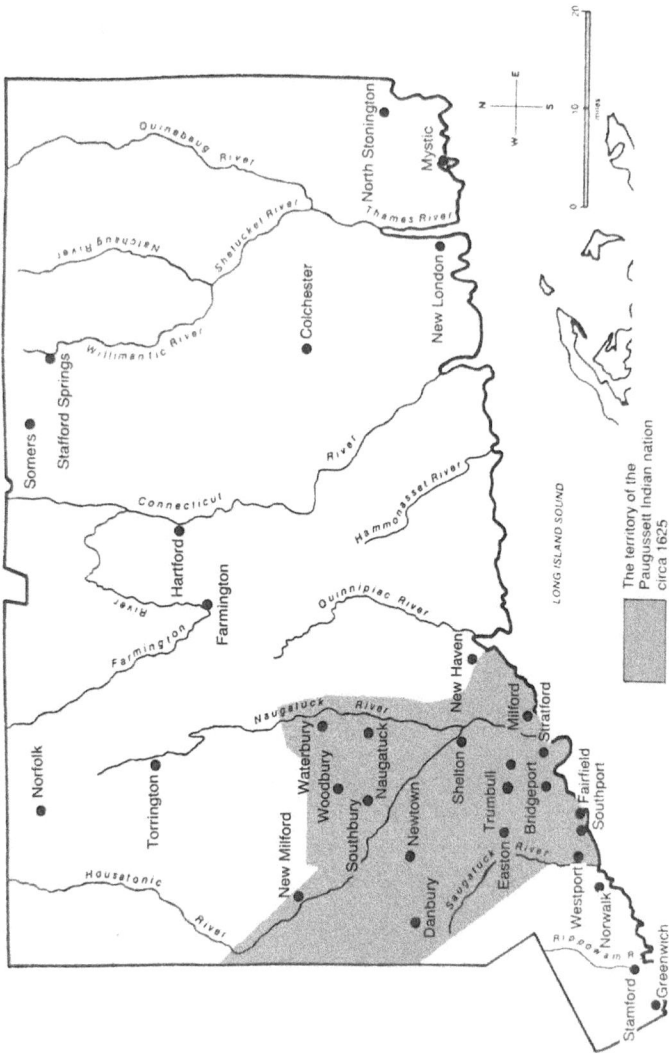

The state of Connecticut, showing major rivers and cities, and the places mentioned by Chief Big Eagle in this book.

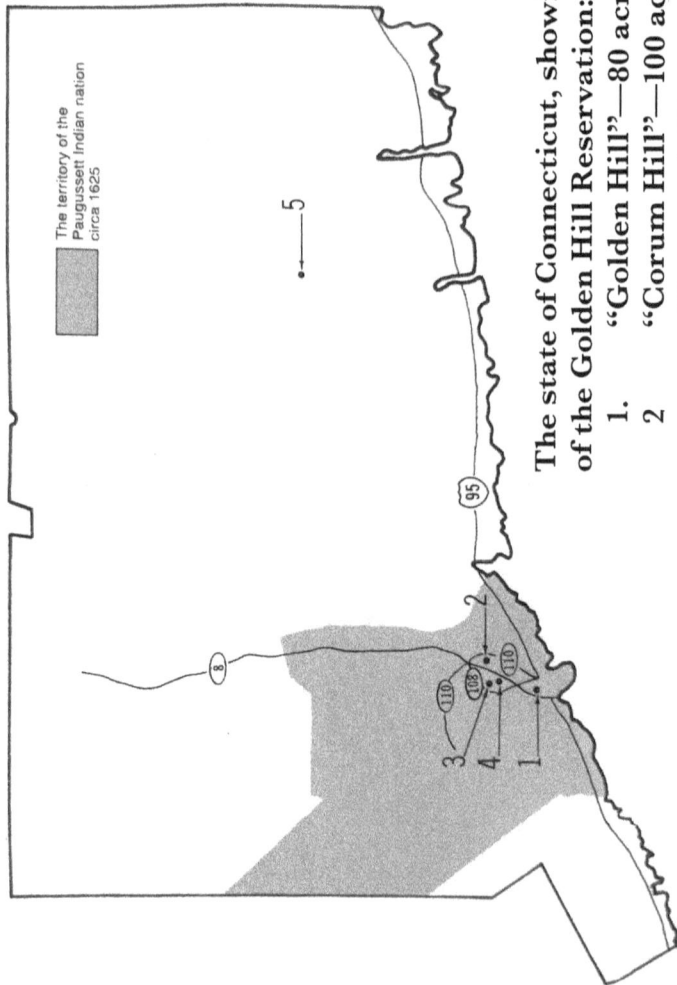

The state of Connecticut, showing the successive sites of the Golden Hill Reservation:

1. "Golden Hill"—80 acres—Bridgeport
2. "Corum Hill"—100 acres—west bank of the Housatonic River
3. "Turkey Meadows"—19¾ acres—Trumbull
4. "Quarter-acre" of Turkey Meadows land repurchased
5. The 69 (later 108) acres—Colchester

The territory of the Paugussett Indian nation circa 1625

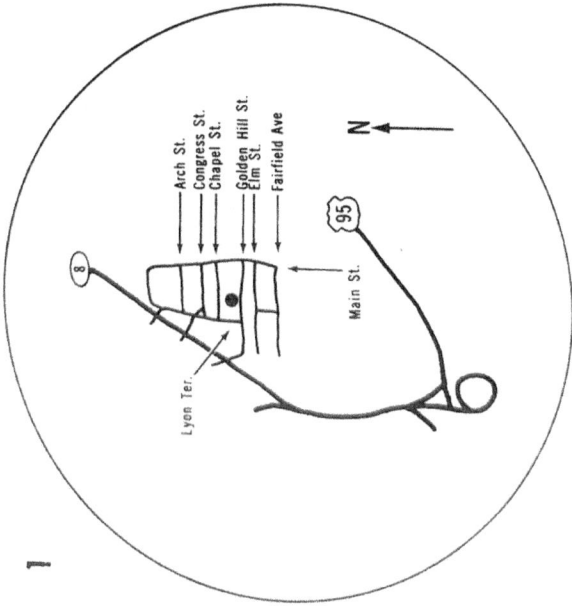

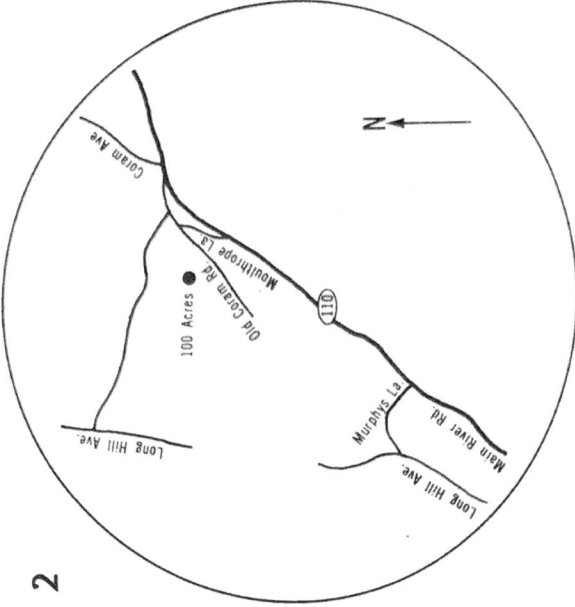

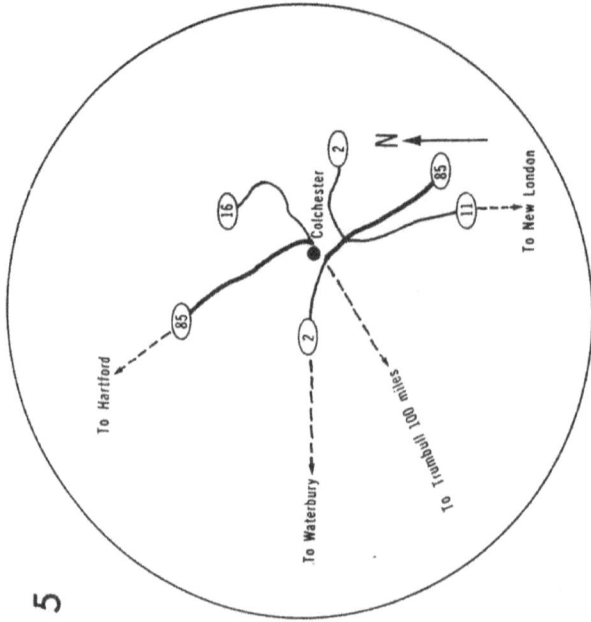

5

To Hartford

85

16

To Waterbury

2

Colchester

2

N

85

11

To Trumbull 100 miles

To New London

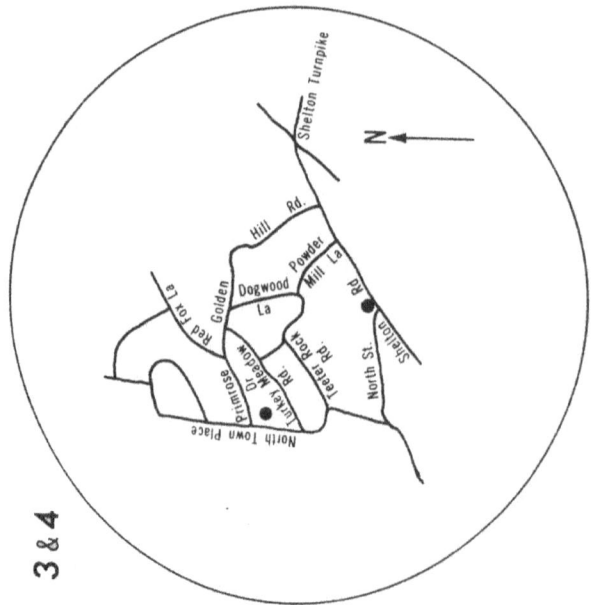

3 & 4

Shelton Turnpike

N

Hill Rd.

Golden

Dogwood La

Powder Mill La

Teeter Rock Rd.

Turkey Meadow Rd.

Primrose Dr.

Red Fox La

North Town Place

North St.

Shelton Rd.

PART II

CHAPTER FIFTEEN

SEVERAL DAYS AFTER I MADE THIS TAPE, I was released from the intensive care unit. I didn't die. And I didn't go home. I went to the state capitol in Hartford, with my former wife, to play my tape for all to hear.

My doctor was upset. He wanted me to go home. But I told him: *Let me worry about the Man Upstairs. All you can do is pull the sheet over my head. When the Creator wants me, he will take me.*

But He didn't want me. So I went to Hartford to deliver my tape. And I told the man at the desk that if they tried to evict me from the reservation, there would be big trouble. So the man left the desk and came back minutes later with six six-foot-tall state troopers. And my wife said: *I only want to give him his medication and water, and I'm going.*

And she left. I don't blame her. She was afraid. But I was committed. Whatever was to happen, was to be. But this wasn't the end. I delivered my tape. And by the end of the month—by the end of March, 1975—the old Sherman homestead had been demolished, and the state was drawing up plans for a new log house.

A few years ago I received a letter from a young student. He wanted to visit the reservation. He wanted *to see Indians living in their native habitat.* That letter broke my heart. What could I tell that student? We have no habitat. The White Man took it.

Even when the land was being protected by the state, the White Man took it. What happened was that the state would appoint an overseer, and the land would end up being owned by his relatives. They'd leave Indian land to their own children.

It was sad. It happened over and over. The overseers would

take ten or fifteen acres to pay a bill for a ton of coal. The Indians needed the coal to keep warm in winter.

The Indian Affairs Coordinator has admitted that he knows very little about the lost land. In his office are records from over three hundred years of relations between the Indian tribes and the state of Connecticut. But those records hardly fill a filing cabinet. No one keeps a record when he steals something.

Somehow records are always destroyed or burned or lost. Let me give you some examples. I served in the U.S. Navy during World War II. I was on the *Thomas Jefferson*, and we came under enemy fire. Ships were tied up in port, riding at anchor, and a submarine turned loose its torpedoes. Suddenly, ships were sinking and the water was full of men. The *Elizabeth C. Scott* went down, sunk. But our captain slipped anchor and we ran to sea.

You don't forget things like that. I served in the Navy, and when I complained about the bad treatment and the prejudice, I was put in the Army. I saw a lot of action, and during the war for this quarter-acre, when my neighbors were demanding that I prove every little detail about myself, I had to verify my service record. So I wrote the General Services Administration, and they wrote back: *We have been unable to locate the record to answer your inquiry. If the record was here on July 12, 1973, it would have been in the area that suffered the most damage in the fire on that date and may have been destroyed.*

My inquiry was about my Army record, but I wasn't supposed to be in the Army. I had served in the Navy. The law says that *any officer knowing that you are erroneously in the service* is responsible for your pay, your welfare, etc. That is why, when I was in the Army, they kept shipping me from place to place. I finally ended up in Burma.

The same thing happened when my lawyers were doing research during the war for this quarter-acre. They couldn't get the records of the previous court cases. I have a letter from a Bridgeport library which states that the material we wanted was *missing or stolen.* But later those records suddenly turned up.

It is always convenient when records are lost. Because there is no evidence of what happened.

Indian records always seem to disappear. Especially when land is involved. What it is is that everybody knows how to take, and nobody knows how to give back. There is no problem with it comes to *selling* Indian land. But to get it back you have to prove every little detail. Or you have to be militant.

It's a hard fact living here. We have had to fight every bit of the way. A quarter-acre is not a native habitat.

That's why I like it in Maine. There is elbow room. Lots of woods for hunting and fishing. Room for dogs and horses. You can drum all you want and nobody complains. I was retired in Maine. But I had to come back home to defend this quarter-acre.

But now it is 1984, and you are hearing a lot about a book by that name, *1984* by George Orwell. It talks about Big Brother. And Big Brother is here and now. Only it's called Big Business. If the government called in all its loans today, you'd have no farmers, no factories, and no people living in rural areas. The government is in control. It is very difficult for Indians to deal with Big Brother to bring about a decent life.

But I have a dream of how life could be for the Paugussetts. If we had enough land, we could live together as a tribe. We could preserve our culture and maintain the natural environment. We could manage the timber and the wildlife. We would need thirty log houses for the Golden Hill tribe. We'd have community gardens and stables and riding trails. We'd have a trading post and a community center and a crafts cooperative. We'd have a place to teach our language to our children.

That would be a native habitat. But it would take a lot of good land.

According to the 1977 census of the Connecticut Indian Affairs Council, there are more than four thousand Indians living in this state. Many of those Indians want to live on reservations now. In the past they had to leave the reservations to get jobs. There was no money on the land. At any one time there were no more than twenty-eight Indians living on the four reservations in Connecticut.

But today, no place in the state is very far away from a city or a job. Indians have jobs and cars and high school diplomas and even college degrees. We can get back to the land if we want to, instead of being scattered all over the place. All it takes is good land.

The log house in which I live belongs to the Golden Hill tribe. I live here because I am Chief Big Eagle. We have an Indian museum in the basement. There are native arts and crafts downstairs. There are relics of my ancestors. I do my beadwork down there.

But there is not enough room for a tribe to gather.

CHAPTER SIXTEEN

NOW I WILL TELL YOU about the war.

The war for this quarter-acre began in the summer of 1976, right in the middle of the American Bicentennial celebration. I was out in Wisconsin at the Munsee Indian Reservation with the curator of the Trailside Museum of the Ward Pond Ridge Reservation in New York. We were tracing the Delaware Indian language. Then I got word that the White neighbor who owns the land next door to the quarter-acre had filed a lawsuit. He claimed that the quarter-acre was his property. He claimed that he had bought the land from George Sherman years ago. He said to *cover over the hole and get the hell off his land.*

The *hole* was the foundation for the log house that was being built on the foundation of the old Sherman homestead. The wreckage of the old home had been cleared away and the state had begun construction on the new log house.

I flew home immediately. I met with members of the tribe. We decided to fight the neighbors by every means possible.

Relations with the neighbors have never been good. Millionaires live around here. This is one of the richest areas in the United States. They don't want an Indian reservation in the back yard. They say it brings the property values down.

Trumbull is supposed to be *sophisticated*. But it is intolerant to anyone but White suburbanites. They say I don't fit in. They don't like my drumming. They don't like my dogs. I have told you about the drumming. And there is a reason for my dogs. It is the same reason why I have a .38 caliber Colt.

I have several dogs tied up out back. German shepherds. They are not for eating, as the old Indian recipe joke implies. They are guard dogs. After I retired from the trucking business, I worked as a security guard for a local bank. I have a permit for my .38 caliber Colt. The dogs and the gun were a part of my job.

I have been a bank guard and driver for the City Trust Company of Bridgeport. I have worked for the Pinkerton Detective Agency. To work for Pinkerton and carry a gun, you have to be trained. You have to be qualified. I also worked for Marine Security in the town of Milford, on the harbor. I have a very good record. In fact, I have a photograph of the Milford Chief of Police awarding me a trophy for the work I did there with the children.

I carried a gun long before the war was declared here. I carried a gun for a living. Today, I hold permits for Maine, Massachusetts, and Connecticut. The dogs and gun were a part of my job. They came in handy during pony shows, when Indians display their crafts. Much of the Indian handiwork and artwork is done with silver. It's very valuable. It has to be protected when the show is over.

But the neighbors complained that the dogs barked. They said I was going to shoot people. They complained that cars blocked their driveways when the tribe gathered for ceremonies. They said we make noise. But when their sons and daughters blast their stereo record players, that is not noise. That is music.

When the war for this quarter-acre began, the neighbors wanted to move me out of here. To get rid of the *riff-raff*, the undesirables.

Downstairs in the tribal museum there is an old real estate advertisement that dates back to the last century. It is an ad for a homestead in this area. The photo shows Nichols Green at the fork in the road not far from here. There were not many houses here then. It looks a lot like it did when I was a boy. That advertisement reads:

Nichols is accessible only by auto or bus or private conveyance, a feature which ensures a good class of people and prevents any chance of cheapening the town by an influx of undesirables.

There's that word again. *Undesirables. Riff-raff.* Indians are always the undesirables.

Not long after I returned to the reservation in 1973, there was an article in the local newspaper about the development of the Woods estate, another piece of local property. There was talk in town of applying to the federal government for money to help finance the project. But it didn't go through. As someone said, *why go through all that trouble only to have Washington give the property to the Blacks?* The same article said that *people in town are bigots.*

And during the war for this quarter-acre, when the head of the Human Rights Agency in Hartford was given money to do a study of this town, the study concluded that Trumbull is one of the worst towns for a minority to live in. I learned of the study when I was trying to get some satisfaction for all the abuse I was taking here in town. The man in charge, a Mr. Green, said that the information was there on file in Hartford, if anyone wanted to look at it.

But not all the neighbors here are bad or difficult. Some have been very helpful. Very sympathetic. Some wrote very positive letters to the newspapers during the war for this quarter-acre, while the others were calling us riff-raff. Some, in fact, wish they could be Indians.

One man told me he wished he could live like me. *You are free,* he said. *My wife wants this and my wife wants that.* Another has a wife that's an alcoholic. Why is she an alcoholic? Because it takes her only fifteen minutes to clean her house. She leads a push-button life.

Many of the teenagers who live around here come home from school each day to find a note on the table. The note says *Go to McDonald's for French fries.* So the kids go to McDonald's for French fries. But soon they get tired of French fries and try marijuana.

The White families that live around here have problems because many of the men work at jobs they hate. They will tell you so. A two-week vacation in the woods each year does them no good. I don't understand how they can live like that. If I had my way, I'd live in the woods all the time.

But some of the neighbors, as I have said, have been very helpful. Very nice. The man who owns the gas station across the street left the restrooms open during the war, so the Indians who were staying on the reservation could have water and use the toilet.

And when it got to the point that we had to patrol the reservation twenty-four hours a day, some of the White neighbors stood guard for us, so we could get a little sleep.

It wasn't always easy for those neighbors to support us. They did it at their own risk. One neighbor, who was very vocal in our support, received obscene phone calls and even a threat of death. It's on record at the Trumbull Police Department.

But these good neighbors continued to help us just the same. They realize that Indians are different, and they can accept that. There is nothing wrong with being different. If everyone was the same, it would be hell.

CHAPTER SEVENTEEN

BEFORE I WENT TO THE MUNSEE RESERVATION in Wisconsin in the summer of 1976, the Indian Affairs Coordinator had received a letter from my White neighbor. In the letter the neighbor claimed that he owned this quarter-acre. But I wasn't told of the letter.

There was a member of the Golden Hill tribe who knew of the letter too. But he said nothing. He assured me that nothing was happening. He is an Indian that has been assimilated into White society. He prefers the ways of the White Man. He knows nothing of true Indian-ness—Indian life and Indian law and Indian ways. He knew of the letter, and he let me leave town.

At one point the White neighbor who was claiming this land offered to trade *his* quarter-acre for state-owned property of equal value. To get something for nothing. At another point he simply offered to *return the land* in order to *benefit the Indians*. But it wasn't his land to return.

So he stopped making offers and challenged the legal title to the quarter-acre. He charged the state of Connecticut with the unlawful demolition of the old Sherman homestead. He said the home had been destroyed without a permit. He stirred things up in a hurry.

And the state, threatened with a lawsuit, ordered a halt to the construction of the log house. They ordered the land to be surveyed. They ordered a title search—a search through all the old records and deeds to determine the rightful owner of this land. I knew who owned this land. The Paugussetts did. But no one would take my word for it. I could have saved them a lot of trouble. But they wouldn't listen to me.

The White neighbor charged us with everything he could think of. At one point, he said the quarter-acre was too small for a proper septic system. The land wasn't large enough to allow for proper drainage of sewage. The Shermans had had a bathroom and a septic system put in and no one had complained. The log house would have a proper bathroom and septic system too. But the neighbor said the property was too small for that. It would be unsanitary. Therefore we couldn't live here. That is what he really meant.

Meanwhile, word of the war got around quickly, and Indians came to support us. We put up a teepee beside the foundation of the log house for the Indians who came from out of town and out of state. The teepee belonged to Jane Deerheart, whose Indian name is Tomkus. The teepee cost over seven hundred dollars, and she let us use it. There was not a lot of room.

When the old homestead was demolished, I had moved into a shed-like building at the left rear corner of the quarter-acre. That shed is still there. It measures fourteen feet by sixteen feet. It was built in 1831, maybe earlier. Originally, it was made of plank boards, like the old homestead. Today, it is covered with gray shingles.

A man named Warner, from one of the state colleges, has dated the shed to at least 1831 because the chimney was built before the use of Portland cement. The shed is made of hand-hewn beams. It is no bigger than a small garage. We used to store old furniture in there. My uncle Ed Sherman had let the neighborhood kids use the shed as a clubhouse. When I returned to the reservation in 1973, kids were in the habit of playing all over this land, bouncing balls off the side of the homestead as if the property belonged to them. But I soon put a stop to that.

I had intended to keep my pony in the shed. But when the old homestead was taken down, that shed became my home. The state offered me a hotel room in Bridgeport, because the Indian Affairs Coordinator claimed that the contractor's insurance would not cover me while the log house was under construction. But I wasn't going to abandon the reservation under any circumstances. So I put my belongings in the hotel room and stayed in the shed.

My neighbor had said the shed was his too.

My son Kenny—Moon Face—moved into the shed with me. My wife left the reservation to stay with relatives. There was no room, and things were heating up. Things were getting unpleasant.

The shed had no central heating, no electricity, no plumbing. We heated it with a propane stove. We had only a wrought-iron bed, an old couch, a bureau, a locker, and a kitchen set. We thought we'd only have to stay in the shed a short time. But we were wrong.

The teepee that was put up held as many as a dozen Indians at a time. Indians slept in the shed when the teepee was full. Sometimes I slept in the teepee myself. It's nice in a teepee. You can't keep too much stuff in there. Just what you need. But it's warm. Even in the winter, when it was covered with snow. It was warm in that teepee.

But the neighbor who was claiming this land said that the teepee was unsanitary. All those Indians living in a teepee. People living in a shed. Cooking food outdoors. The neighbor claimed it was unsanitary and immoral and indecent. All of America camps out in its own back yard, but when an Indian does it, it's indecent.

The Indians who stayed in the teepee did so to show their support. They came from as far away as Canada. When the AIM joined the fight, the brothers of AIM stayed in the teepee too.

And I want to make one thing clear. During the war for this quarter-acre, the tribes of Connecticut did not support us, not with food, nor with wood to keep us warm through the winter, nor by appearing at the reservation. One or two Connecticut Indians did support us as individuals, but their tribes did not. The Indian tribes of Connecticut did not back or support the Golden Hill people in our fight to save this quarter-acre. They did not want us on the Indian Affairs Council, and they did not care if we lost our land.

CHAPTER EIGHTEEN

A TITLE SEARCH COSTS MONEY. People have to be paid to go through all the existing legal records. They have to trace the records back as far as they go. Surveyors cost money. Lawyers cost money too.

The White neighbor who was taking us to court didn't have to worry about a lawyer. His daughter is a lawyer. He himself is a lawyer and a local politician. He knows people. He knows how to use the law. He knew how to get around the local zoning laws to develop the land. He wanted to develop the land behind the reservation.

I have a tape recording of a meeting of the historical society in Trumbull, a meeting that was taped by people from *The New York Times*. On that tape you can hear a lady say, *There is a developer offering $34,000 an acre for the swamp land*. The *swamp land* is the wet land behind the reservation, the former Indian land of Turkey Meadows.

Later in that same meeting someone said, *The going price for Golden Hill is $450,000 cash on the barrel head*. That part is not on the tape, but I have a witness from that meeting. Nearly half a million dollars for that land.

If you sold that land for $34,000 an acre and put a $200,000 house on it, you'd be a millionaire in no time. The land around here is very valuable, so you can understand why it was necessary to determine the proper owner.

But the Paugussetts had no money to fight the neighbor's claim to the quarter-acre. So we set up the Golden Hill Defense Fund. To raise money for legal fees. During the course of the war I spoke at many places to help raise funds. I spoke at Yale University. I spoke at Fairfield University. I spoke at colleges and universities and high schools. Each time I spoke, I told our story. I told our history and what was happening to us.

I told these audiences that the eastern Indians are officially non-existent. They receive no assistance from the United States government, unlike our western brothers. And the Constitution of the United States says, in Article VI: *This Constitution; and the laws of the United States which shall be made in pursuance thereof; and all Treaties which shall be made under the Authority of the United States, shall be the supreme Law of the Land.*

And Article I, section VIII, says that the Congress of the United States *shall have the power to regulate commerce with foreign nations, and among the several states, and with the Indian tribes.* Indians are the only one of today's minorities mentioned in the Constitution of the United States. All treaties and agreements made with the Indians are supposed to be the supreme law of the land. But they have been broken. They have not been honored. Why?

The United States Department of the Interior used to say that these agreements were made with the thirteen original colonies, and that is why the tribes were not federally recognized. When the thirteen colonies became states, the Indians west of the Mississippi River were made charges of the states. Each state kept its Indians unto itself, without the federal government as a partner. So the government had an excuse for not recognizing us, for not helping us. But based on deeds issued by the government of the thirteen original colonies, the Paugussetts could actually lay claim to the entire city of Bridgeport!

That is what I told them. I told our story over and over, to make money for our legal expenses. I told them that the Golden Hill tribe is not federally recognized. Therefore we receive no help from the Bureau of Indian Affairs in Washington, D.C. That bureau was set up in 1824 as a branch of the War Department to deal with the Indians out west. They certainly put it in the right department, because Indians have been making war ever since. But the Bureau of Indian Affairs would have nothing to do with the war for this quarter-acre.

I know of only one tribe east of the Mississippi that does get special recognition by the United States government. The

Penobscots of Maine. Why is that? Because Senator Muskie took up their cause. But if you look at the voting records of the senators from Connecticut, whenever there is an Indian issue they cry *No! No! No!*

This is what I told any audience that would listen, for whatever they could pay. I said these things over and over. And then we got a break. We got some famous people to take up our cause.

The first came in October 1976. The title search was dragging on. The construction of the log house was halted. I was living in the shed. Other Indians were living in the teepee. Then Mr. William Kunstler came to the reservation. He was in Connecticut for a trial in Waterbury. He had been informed of our trouble. Mr. Kunstler is a famous lawyer, a nationally known civil rights attorney. And he came to this quarter-acre.

Mr. Kunstler is a very dignified man. Very smart and very calm. We showed him the reservation. We showed him the foundation of the log house, and the teepee, and the shed. There were about two hundred people here, coming and going all day. There were many newspaper reporters too.

And here is what Mr. Kunstler said. I made a tape recording of his remarks. It was October 29, 1976. In the background of the tape you can hear the drums beating. Heavy, plodding drumbeats. The heartbeat of my ancestors. And there are Indians singing. You would call it chanting. It is almost like crying: *Ki yi yi yi. Ki yi yi yi.* There is drumming on the tape and the Indians singing, and then Mr. Kunstler speaks:

I just want to say a few words about the legal aspects of this case. The reason why Chief Big Eagle is doing this and why we're all here. The teepee, of course, is traditional to Native American life. The teepee was put here because the state has stopped building the structure which is just ahead of us there, because the lawyer who lives next door has sent a letter claiming he owns the land. However, the deed to this property goes back at least to 1876, when the land was bought by the great-grandfather of Chief Big Eagle. And then in 1886, I believe, it was deeded to Roland Lacy, who was the Indian agent, to be held forever in trust for the Golden Hill tribe of the Paugussett nation. And so the land, for at least one hundred years, has been either in direct ownership of Native Americans or held in trust by virtue of a deed which I have here. The deed is dated February 5, 1886, from

William Sherman, great-grandfather of Mr. Piper, to Roland Lacy, agent of the Golden Hill tribe of Indians.

The state started the log structure after tearing down the one that had been here. Then it stopped building, for at least since July, on the theory that the neighbor has made a claim, and therefore they are not going to build until they check out that claim and the title to the land. In August it was assigned out for title checking and now we're into the end of October, and there's no report that I know of that's been made, although I understand that the report's going to show that at least for one hundred years this land is as I have described it.

And now winter is approaching and the structure is still not up. The reason for putting the teepee up is that there is an old regulation or law that says, in order to hold this land in trust, the Native Americans must live on it two months of the year. And so the teepee was put up to provide a place where people will live to consummate those two months, because the original tract of land that was given to the Golden Hill people in the 1600s had a provision on it that they must remain on the land; that if they ever left the land, the land could be given back or taken by the state of Connecticut, or by the Colony of Connecticut originally. And so the teepee is up now in order to make that two months' possibility of living on the land, so there is no chance of saying that there's no member of the Golden Hill tribe here, because then the land would be taken over by the state of Connecticut, as was all of the land which belonged to Native Americans in this part of the world.

I'm glad to be here because this is an eastern tribe, not a western tribe. I've been associated mainly with western tribes, namely the Plains Indians, people who were driven from the east coast by the advancing White invaders. But this is essentially where it all began, on the east coast, the attack that drove Native Americans across this country until they met the invaders from the west coast, and stayed in the Plains states where the last resistance occurred, resistance which ended with the massacre at Wounded Knee in 1890.

So I am offering my services to do what we can to see that the log house is built and that the smallest reservation in the United States remains intact, because it is a symbolic place, the place of the beginning, symbolic of what the White people did to the Native Americans who befriended the first settlers, only to find that they had welcomed into their midst the people who would try to destroy them.

I'm going to be a part of this case until we get the house built and safeguard this place from being taken over and destroyed. But what's more important is that the lawyers and the people who are here today demonstrate their solidarity by whatever legal means possible. The people have come out to demonstrate their solidarity with the Golden Hill tribe, which at one time resided where all of downtown Bridgeport is today. And now this tribe is down to this quarter-acre, which is the last remnant of the Indian landlords of this country, who owned all of the land before it was stripped from them.

CHAPTER NINETEEN

THAT IS WHAT MR. KUNSTLER SAID. Then he returned to Waterbury, but he remained on the team of lawyers that was helping us.

When the civil rights movement was just beginning, Mr. Kunstler worked on cases of racial discrimination. He defended the famous Chicago Seven, who were charged with disrupting the 1968 Democratic National Convention. He has helped many civil rights laws to be passed. He helped the Indians out west and he came here to help *us*, and his appearance served to get things rolling.

Mr. Kunstler mentioned that the claim to this property goes back at least to 1876. But it goes back much farther than that.

Down in the basement museum I have a diary that belonged to my great-grandfather, William Sherman. It covers the years from 1848 to 1877. It tells everything that William Sherman did on the days that he lived on this land. In the diary is a note from an Indian agent which shows that Indians were living on this property for at least sixty years before it was first purchased. Indians have been buried on this land. You can read in the diary where my great-grandfather *went to Bridgeport to get a casket*. Everybody around here knew this was a reservation.

The diary records the life of William Sherman. It lists the people he worked for—families like the Amblers, the Curtises, the Nothnagles, the Plums. Here is a sample of that diary for the month of July 1876. In that month Americans were celebrating their Centennial. America was one hundred years old. And one hundred years later, during the Bicentennial, when America was two hundred years old, they would try to take away this land.

July 1876

July 1	*Saturday*	*haying*
July 2	*Sunday*	*at home, fixed Martinsburg cradle*
July 3	*Monday*	*haying*
July 4	*Tuesday*	*haying*
July 5	*Wednesday*	*haying*
July 6	*Thursday*	*haying 9 hours*
July 7	*Friday*	*haying*
July 8	*Saturday*	*finished haying*
July 9	*Sunday*	*at home*
July 10	*Monday*	*went to Stratford*
July 11	*Tuesday*	*moved and carted bedding*
July 12	*Wednesday*	*sold turnips*
July 13	*Thursday*	*went to get ox*
July 14	*Friday*	*turnpike ½ day*
July 15	*Saturday*	*plowed ½ day, very hot*
July 16	*Sunday*	*at home*
July 17	*Monday*	*plowed all day*
July 18	*Tuesday*	*plowed ½ day*
July 19	*Wednesday*	*plowed ½ day*
July 20	*Thursday*	*at home, very hot*
July 21	*Friday*	*plowed all day*
July 22	*Saturday*	*plowed all day*
July 23	*Sunday*	*at home, cleaned well*
July 24	*Monday*	*plowed all day*
July 25	*Tuesday*	*plowed all day*
July 26	*Wednesday*	*finished plowing, fixed wagon*
July 27	*Thursday*	*carted wood*
July 28	*Friday*	*cut brush ½ day*
July 29	*Saturday*	*went a-clamming*
July 30	*Sunday*	*at home*
July 31	*Monday*	*grinding all day*

The turnpike mentioned on July 14 was the Wells Hollow Turnpike. Today it is the Shelton Road. William Sherman worked on that road, and the diary shows that he sent his sons to work on that road because it was passing through reservation land. Other pages of the diary record the following things that my great-grandfather did: *picking up stone, digging stone, stoning well, digging ditch, stoning ditch, spreading manure, making fence, planting corn, cutting corn, chopping wood, carting wood, stripping trees, cutting and drawing hogs, hole-ing posts, cutting beef, hoeing potatoes, setting out onions, tending hens and turkeys, carting gravel, mending baskets.*

There was a regular farm operating on this land, and it took more than just a quarter-acre. I have a photograph of a fruit stand that my grandfather, George Sherman, used to run here. All of the produce for that stand came off this land. We used to have a barn back in the woods by where a woman has a tennis court today. You used to be able to see electric wires running through the woods. They went right to the barn. I can remember when we were still using all that land behind the quarter-acre. As a boy, I used to ride my pony all over it.

The diary shows some other important things too. In the fall of 1875, my great-grandfather began recording entries he called *work on my house.* That house was the old Sherman homestead. He had been working on it long before this land was officially set aside by the state as a reservation in 1886. While building the homestead, William Sherman lived in the shed I have described, where I lived during the war for this quarter-acre.

Work on my house, 1875

Oct. 1	Friday	got timber from Ambler's woods
Oct. 2	Saturday	timber to shed
Oct. 3	Sunday	at home
Oct. 4	Monday	well ½ dug
Oct. 5	Tuesday	finished shaving timber
Oct. 6	Wednesday	stormy, had a lame ox
Oct. 7	Thursday	got a load of lumber
Oct. 8	Friday	got a load of lumber
Oct. 9	Saturday	got oil and paint pails
Oct. 10	Sunday	at home
Oct. 11	Monday	got brick, rainy
Oct. 12	Tuesday	began digging cellar

Oct. 13	*Wednesday*	*digging cellar*
Oct. 14	*Thursday*	*digging cellar*
Oct. 15	*Friday*	*finished digging cellar*
Oct. 16	*Saturday*	*fixed barrels for Ambler*
Oct. 17	*Sunday*	*at home*
Oct. 18	*Monday*	*in cellar, Ike Curtis to help*
Oct. 19	*Tuesday*	*in cellar*
Oct. 20	*Wednesday*	*fixed bridge, got load sand*
Oct. 21	*Thursday*	*spent ½ day in cellar*
Oct. 22	*Friday*	*in cellar*
Oct. 23	*Saturday*	*in cellar*
Oct. 24	*Sunday*	*at home*
Oct. 25	*Monday*	*in cellar*
Oct. 26	*Tuesday*	*work in cellar*
Oct. 27	*Wednesday*	*went to Bridgeport for lime & brick*
Oct. 28	*Thursday*	*bricked house*
Oct. 29	*Friday*	*worked on house*
Oct. 30	*Saturday*	*went to Bridgeport*
Oct. 31	*Sunday*	*at home*
Nov. 1	*Monday*	*worked on house*
Nov. 2	*Tuesday*	*worked on house*
Nov. 3	*Wednesday*	*worked on house*
Nov. 4	*Thursday*	*brought hay up to house*
Nov. 5	*Friday*	*stoned cellar*
Nov. 6	*Saturday*	*went to Bridgeport, got windows*
Nov. 7	*Sunday*	*at home*
Nov. 8	*Monday*	*½ day on house*
Nov. 9	*Tuesday*	*moved*
Nov. 10	*Wednesday*	*packed, rained*
Nov. 11	*Thursday*	*finished moving*

Then, on January 13, 1876, two months after the last entry above, my great-grandfather records: *Went to Bridgeport, got money to pay for house, $200.* You notice he did *not* say *borrowed money from bank or Indian agent.* In those days we had tribal funds. I have some of the old bank books. And according to the diary, William Sherman was making good money: *$1, ½ day* and *$2, all day.*

At that same period of time, the soldiers of the United States Army, who were fighting the Navajo and Sioux out west, were earning less than twenty dollars a month. But my ancestors were not out west scalping people, raiding stagecoaches, or robbing trains. They were right here, working the land. That is what the diary shows.

People have claimed that Indians were always too lazy to work, that we were always drunk, never clean. They say we were always on welfare. But we can't have been too desperate. You have to wonder how a man like my great-grandfather could have been on welfare. He was a smart Indian. He earned good money. And he built a homestead on this quarter-acre of land.

CHAPTER TWENTY

BESIDES MR. KUNSTLER, some other famous people helped us too. Not famous lawyers, but people famous for *breaking* the law. They were Clyde Bellecourt, Russell Means, and John Thomas—nationally known Indian activists. They came to help us raise money for the Golden Hill Defense Fund. And they were ready to fight, if necessary.

In December of 1890, United States troopers killed three hundred Sioux Indians—men, women, and children—in a battle at Wounded Knee, South Dakota. The Sioux were wiped out like the Pequots, like the Narragansetts in King Philip's War. But they went down fighting. Wounded Knee was the last Indian massacre in American history. The last Indian resistance. Mr. Kunstler spoke of it when he was here.

In February of 1973, two hundred and fifty Indians went to Wounded Knee again. They went to the Pine Ridge Indian Reservation there. They brought weapons with them. They took some White hostages, and they declared the area free of White control. Clyde Bellecourt and Russell Means were among those Indians. They set up roadblocks and held Wounded Knee for seventy-one days. They held out against a siege by the United States marshals, the FBI, and the local police. They wanted to call the attention of the world to the problems of Native Americans.

They demanded Senate hearings. They demanded a review of Indian treaties. They demanded a review of the handling of Indian affairs. The occupation of Wounded Knee helped to strengthen the American Indian Movement.

Clyde Bellecourt is a Chippewa. He has been to prison, and he has learned from that. He has dedicated his life to helping other Indians stay *out* of prison. Russell Means is an Oglala Sioux. He was raised on the Pine Ridge Indian Reservation in South Dakota. He attended five colleges but never graduated. He had other things to do.

On Thanksgiving Day in 1970, Russell Means helped seize the ship called the *Mayflower II*. In 1971 he occupied Mount Rushmore. In 1972 he occupied the offices of the Bureau of Indian Affairs in Washington, D.C. Occupying the Pine Ridge Reservation at Wounded Knee was a homecoming for him. He organized these demonstrations to call attention to Indian problems.

The American Indian Movement was founded by two Chippewa Indians—George Mitchell and Dennis Banks—in 1968. Clyde Bellecourt and Russell Means helped AIM get national attention. AIM was founded because nothing was being done by the United States government to protect Indian reservations. Nothing was being done to protect Indian culture and Indian land. AIM gave Native Americans a new-found pride in their own identity. AIM is committed to supporting any Indian organization or family. Since 1968 it has helped Indians regain millions of lost acres.

AIM is determined that Native Americans will survive. AIM fights to eliminate racial stereotypes—like John Wayne and his Comancheros—that still influence the treatment of Indians today. AIM works to preserve the spiritual basis of Indian life. AIM fights to hold our hunting and fishing rights, our rights to self-determination and control of our own affairs.

I am a member of AIM. And my AIM brothers—Clyde Bellecourt and Russell Means—came here during the war for this quarter-acre. They came with other Indians from AIM to help protect this reservation. One of them was John Thomas, a Sioux, who later in life helped to carry the mail to Iran during the hostage crisis.

They declared a showdown and they came to fight.

The reporters came out again. And about forty Indians. It was a chilly morning,

November 17, 1976. Clyde Bellecourt was wearing a jeans jacket with an AIM monogram. His hair was pulled into a braid at the side of his head. Russell Means had his hair parted in the middle and pulled back into two braids behind his square face. He wore a shiny windbreaker and his dark eyes were hidden behind reflecting sunglasses.

There was drumming in the background, and singing, just like when Mr. Kunstler was here. And Clyde Bellecourt said, *At Wounded Knee Native Americans died for the land that was sacred to them, to stop the land theft. . . That same kind of commitment is being made to Chief Big Eagle.*

Russell Means drew a parallel between the Indian situation and the systematic extermination of the Jews in World War II. *If the state continues to act like Nazis,* he said, *the only recourse left is to fight for existence.* He said that the case of the Golden Hill Indians is a perfect example of Indians *holding on by their fingernails to their being as a people.* He said Indians are victims of *colonial land-grab mentality* and are faced with cultural genocide. He said that Indians are both *indigenous,* meaning we are native people, and *indigent,* meaning we are poor.

Native Americans are the most deprived and isolated minority in the United States. There are fewer than one million of us, and on every scale of measurement—employment, income, education, and health—we rank at the bottom.

Russell Means said we needed money for the lawyers and surveyors and title search. And he helped us raise that money. Later, when he spoke with me at Yale, there was a crowd of four hundred people at the law school, including Indians from Maine, Massachusetts, and Canada. Russell Means told these people that the Golden Hill land battle is *the most blatant example of greed he has ever seen.* He said, *the vast majority of Americans are completely ignorant of Native Americans—of the forced separation of families, the low life expectancy, and the high rate of alcoholism and suicide.* He said, *these conditions occur because Americans have neglected the Indians after the settlers took their lands.*

And the land is still in danger. But Indians are fighting back. Indians are learning the White Man's law to hold him to broken treaties. But learning the law is difficult because, until very recently, none of the law schools even treated Indian law. Indians were sent from the reservations to the law schools and came back empty-handed. Even the Dean of Harvard Law School has admitted that there are no lawyers qualified to take these Indian cases to court.

So there is nothing to do but fight. And Russell Means and Clyde Bellecourt came here to fight. They had experienced violent confrontations before, and they were ready for anything.

I was committed too. I had fought for this country in World War II. And if I could go over to North Africa to fight somebody I didn't even know, I could stand and fight right here. For my people's land and their right to exist.

CHAPTER TWENTY-ONE

NOW I WANT TO TALK about some of the legal aspects of this case. Some of the laws that applied.

One of the lawyers for the Golden Hill tribe was David Crosby. He was working for Pine Tree Legal Assistance, an organization that is based in Maine. I had known Mr. Crosby in Maine. Pine Tree Legal Assistance has helped many Indians regain their land. Mr. Crosby advised us to let the White neighbor take us to court. He said he would try to get back the nineteen and three-quarter acres we originally owned here in Turkey Meadows, in addition to proving that the quarter-acre belonged to the Paugussetts.

One way to claim the land is by *aboriginal title*. Aboriginal title means that native people have property rights over lands that they have traditionally used and occupied from time immemorial. Land they have held for as far back as anyone can remember. A native claim is based on aboriginal title if any treaties that were made are questionable. Or if treaties were never made. Or if people weren't conquered in war.

And the Paugussetts were never *conquered in war*. In 1637 when the English massacred the Pequots, we didn't fight. We just helped the Pequots who tried to escape. Later, we were given a reservation that was recognized by the Connecticut Colony.

According to Mr. Crosby, two other claims were possible besides *aboriginal title*. One was based on a federal law, the other was based on a state law.

The Federal Non-Intercourse Act of 1790 forbids the sale of Indian land without the approval of the Congress of the United States. That law reads: *No purchase, grant, lease or other conveyance of lands, or of any title or claim thereto, from any Indian nation or tribe of Indians, shall be of any validity in law or equity, unless the same be made by treaty or convention entered into pursuant to the Constitution.*

And in a famous case involving the Seneca Indians, George Washington interpreted just what this law means: *Here, then, is the security for the remainder of your lands . . . the General Government will never consent to your being defrauded, but it will protect you in all your just rights . . . Besides the before mentioned security for your land, you will perceive, by the law of Congress for regulating trade and intercourse with the Indian tribes, the fatherly care the United States intend to take of the Indians.*

The attitude of *fatherly care* disappeared long ago, but we are sure of one thing—the land of the Golden Hill Indians was never taken with federal approval.

A Paugussett by the name of Eliza Wimpy, and other Paugussett tribal members who later went to join the Oneida tribes in New York, filed a claim years ago based on this federal law. They claimed that the Golden Hill people owned the city of Bridgeport. They filed suits for *rents, leases, and damages.* They tried to make the White Man pay for taking Indian land.

That case went nowhere. There was that catch about the original treaties being made with the thirteen colonies. So the 1790 claim was never settled. We thought we might argue it again because it is clear today that the 1790 law applies. But a group called the Native American Rights Fund—NARF—which supports Pine Tree Legal Assistance, wouldn't argue our case based on that claim. Tom Tureen, a lawyer for NARF, said that *Bridgeport is a ninety-million-dollar corporation.* NARF didn't want to go up against it.

Another reason NARF didn't want to back us was because we were ready to use force. We were ready to fight for this quarter-acre if we had to.

Then there is an old Connecticut law that forbids the sale of Indian land without the approval of the state General Assembly. During the title search for this quarter-acre, our lawyer David Crosby said that most of the deeds, when turned up, would *fail to comply* with this state law.

The property that our White neighbor owns next door was purchased from a woman by the name of Sadie McGee. The neighbor claimed that the property he bought from her included the reservation. George Sherman had once deeded the reservation to Sadie McGee. He was the chief of the Paugussetts in those days. But the chief does not have the right to sell land that belongs to the tribe. The land cannot be sold without permission by one member of the tribe.

Sadie McGee was George Sherman's girlfriend. He deeded this quarter-acre to her, but she deeded it back because the original transaction was null and void by law.

Mr. Tureen said, *It's possible that anyone now holding land, even if he bought it in good faith from a succession of non-Indian holders, would be forced to give it back, but this is an area of the law where there are few precedents.*

The law has not been tested enough to depend on it in cases such as ours. And that is the situation with many of the laws. Many were being tested by the Golden Hill tribe. This will help Indian cases in the future, but it made things very difficult for us during the war for this quarter-acre.

Another Connecticut law says that the State has no authority to sell tribal land, and that any profits from the sale of Indian land cannot be used to pay the debts of individual Indians. The state cannot own or sell tribal land. This fact became important when it came to ending the legal battle for the reservation land. But that was eight years after the time I am speaking of now.

We knew that an honest title search would show that the Paugussetts own far more of the state of Connecticut than just this quarter-acre. We own everything else around here for miles. The old stone house on our neighbor's property next door was built by my grandfather. My grandfather built other homes around here too, plus the barn that used to be back in the woods. But we no longer own these buildings.

We knew that an honest title search would show in our favor. And it did. The Indian agents to whom my great-grandfather had signed over the deed to this quarter-acre had never signed off the deed. The property had gone to the state, to be held in trust for the tribe, intact.

And some of the earliest deeds to the property next door

revealed a funny pattern. The earliest record shows the property as *one acre*. Later deeds also show *one acre*. But later still, the deeds begin to read *one acre more or less*. And then *two acres*. So you can see that the reservation land was being taken little by little.

One of the guidelines that surveyors used in measuring the reservation land was a stone wall that runs across the back at the edge of the woods. But they always began measuring from a pile of rocks in the corner behind the shed. In the past those rocks were never there. I have photographs to prove it. There is a difference between a stone wall and a pile of rocks. We were going to bring the judge and jury out here to make that clear.

But the court supported us. The title search proved that the quarter-acre belongs to the Golden Hill people of the Paugussett nation. Forever.

And at the end of November in 1976, just in time for Thanksgiving—a popular White Man's feast founded by Native Americans—the Governor of Connecticut called to tell us that the construction of the log house would resume.

Aurelius Piper poses in his naval uniform at a studio in Tanzania in 1942, prior to the invasion of North Africa. He later served in the United States Army as well. *Photo courtesy of Chief Big Eagle.*

This snapshot from the Sherman family album shows the old Sherman homestead (right) circa 1915. Produce for sale at "GRANPA'S STORE ON RES" was grown on land surrounding the quarter-acre. *Photo courtesy of Chief Big Eagle.*

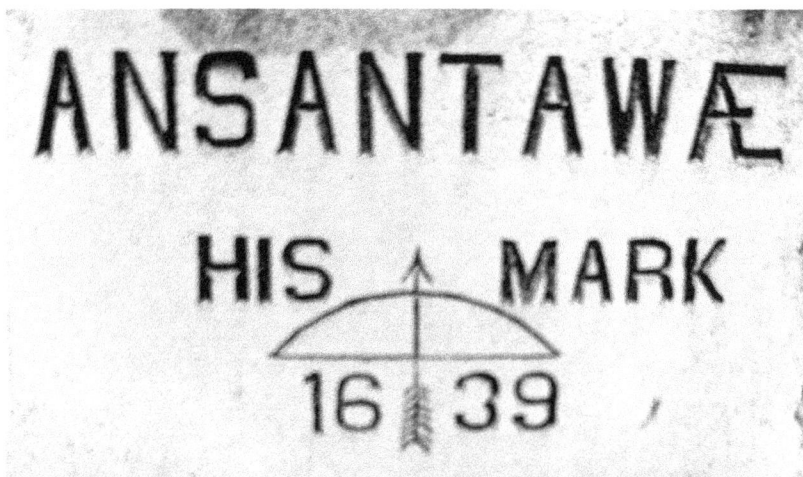

This cornerstone on a bridge over the Wepawaug River in Milford, Connecticut, records the mark of Ansantaway, sachem of the Wepawaugs, one of the five tribes of the Paugussett confederacy. *Photo by C.C. Smith.*

The old Sherman homestead awaits demolition in 1975 to make room for the tribe's state-built log house. Tarpaper was added to the original plank boards, then covered with aluminum siding. Except for a bathroom that was added when the house was ninety years old, the interior remained untouched. *Photo courtesy of Chief Big Eagle.*

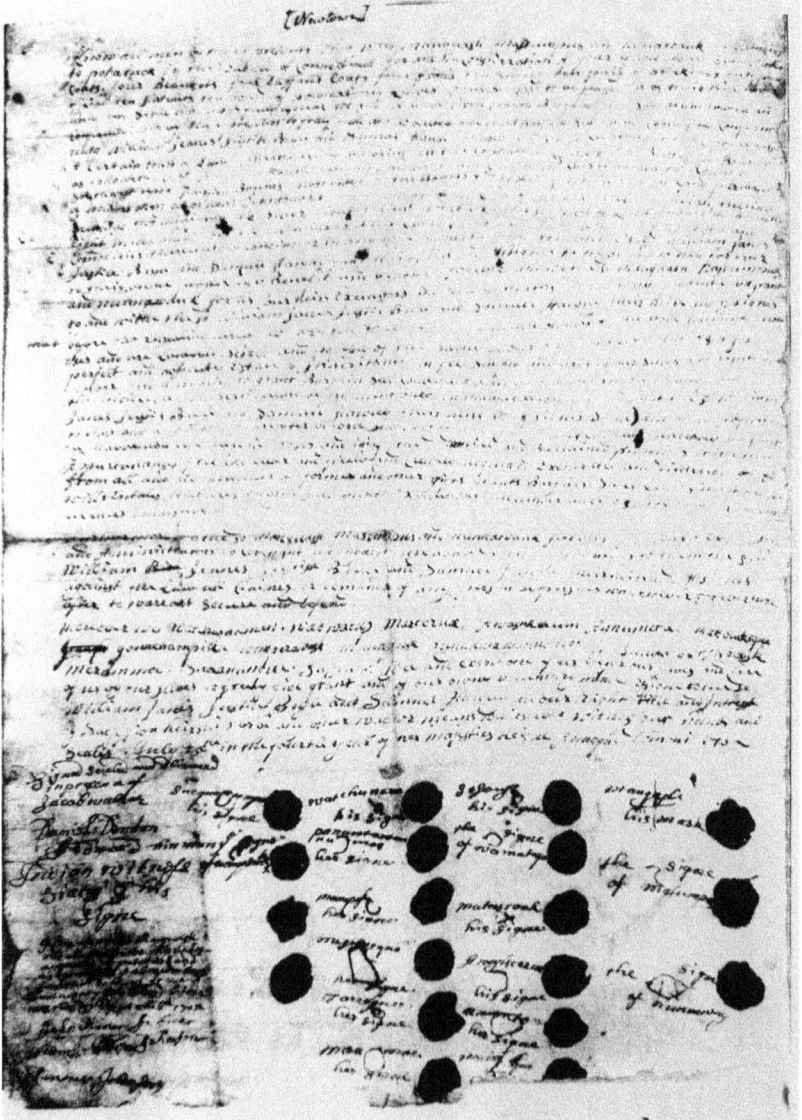

The mark of Ansantaway appears (bottom right) on this 1705 deed in which Paugussett territory was sold to Newtown, Connecticut, for coats, blankets, shirts, and similar articles. The Indians never understood the white man's concept of owning land. *Photocopy of document provided by Chief Big Eagle.*

Noted civil rights attorney William Kunstler joins Chief Big Eagle on the reservation in late October 1976. Kunstler's support helped to call national attention to the case of the Golden Hill Indians. *Photo by John Harvey, courtesy of The Trumbull Times.*

When a neighbor's claim to the quarter-acre halted construction of the log house, Chief Big Eagle moved into a teepee on the property in order to ensure that the reservation was legally occupied. First story of the stone house behind the teepee was built by Chief Big Eagle's grandfather. *Photo by John Harvey, courtesy of The Trumbull Times.*

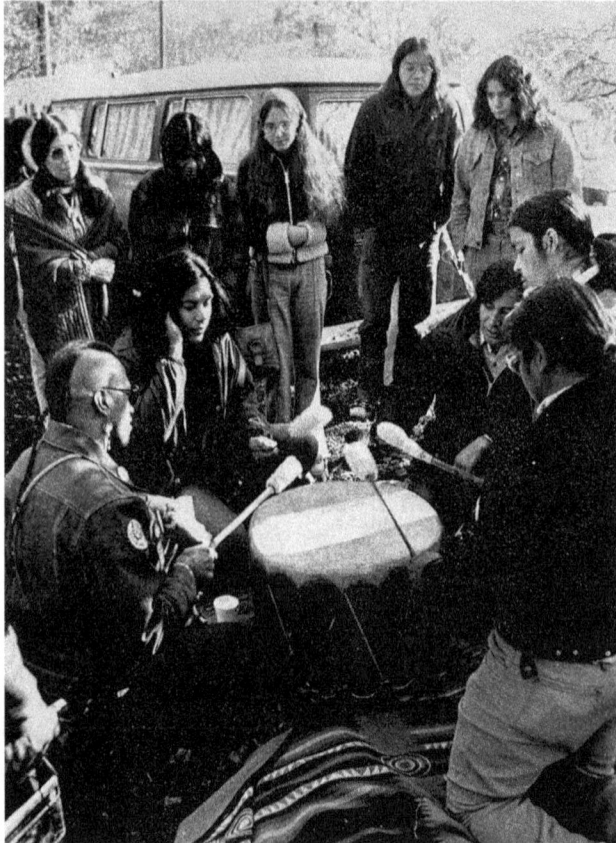

Tall Oak (front left), a Narragansett from Rhode Island, leads the drumming as Indians gather on the reservation in support of the Golden Hill Tribe. Other Indians came from Maine, Wisconsin, and Canada. *Photo by John Harvey, courtesy of The Trumbull Times.*

Braving the winter conditions, sixteen-year-old Moon Face Bear (Kenneth Piper), son of Chief Big Eagle, exits the teepee on the Golden Hill Reservation. Moon Face Bear stayed with his father during the title search and construction of the log house. *Photo courtesy of Chief Big Eagle.*

Brothers of the American Indian Movement (AIM)—Russell Means, Chief Big Eagle, John Thomas, and Clyde Bellecourt (left to right)—take their stand in the foundation of the log house in November of 1976, awaiting results of a title search to determine rightful ownership of the quarter-acre. *Photo courtesy of The Bridgeport Post.*

Somber Indians gather on the reservation beyond the charred remains of the teepee. Chief Big Eagle then moved into the shed in the background. The arson case was never solved. *Photo by John Harvey, courtesy of The Trumbull Times.*

The log house nears completion in the winter of 1977. A second teepee was erected on the reservation for Indian supporters. *Photo courtesy of Chief Big Eagle.*

Chief Big Eagle shares a thought with Indian lawyer Thomas Tureen during the Third Annual Native American Day ceremonies held in Westport, Connecticut, in May of 1977. Tureen viewed the case of the Golden Hill Indians as a test of the American legal system. *Photo by Bill Romei, courtesy of The Trumbull Times.*

Josephine Pirozzoli (right) of the Connecticut Friends of Indians chats with a visitor on the front porch of the completed log home. Mrs. Pirozzoli organized the open house and housewarming activities. *Photo by John Harvey, courtesy of The Trumbull Times.*

Items on view in the basement museum of the log home include the outfit worn by Chief Black Hawk in turn-of-the-century "wild west" shows, an Indian doll on a piece of log from construction materials of the new home (note turtle carved on log), Chief Big Eagle's *gustoweha*, a ceramic owl and an Iroquois water drum (on shelf), a pin cushion (far left), encased owl wing, and a turtle shell rattle. *Photo by C.C. Smith.*

Whites and Indians alike view the handicrafts and artifacts on display in the completed log house during the Golden Hill housewarming celebration. *Photo courtesy of Chief Big Eagle.*

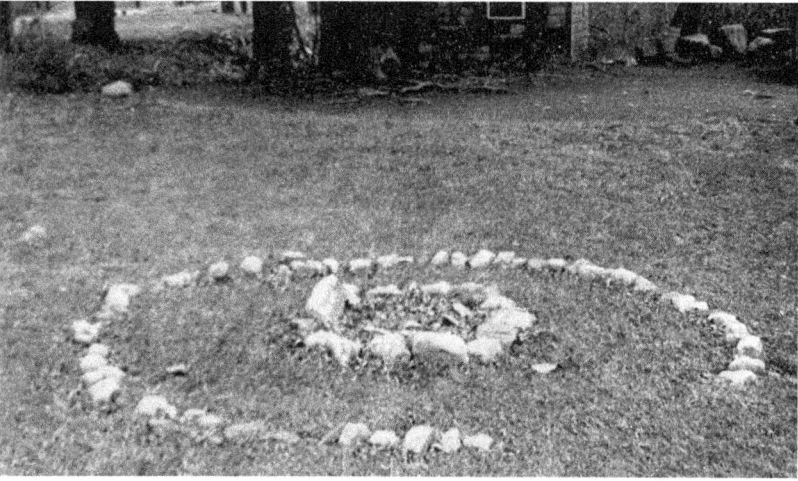

A ceremonial stone fire circle now occupies the site of the burned teepee. *Photo courtesy of Chief Big Eagle.*

Behind the log house on the quarter-acre reservation sits the sweat lodge, which is used in purification ceremonies. Sticks in foreground serve as an altar for the medicine man. *Photo by C.C. Smith.*

Wearing his *gustoweha* and ceremonial ghost-dance shirt, Chief Big Eagle receives a trophy from William Bull, Chief of the Milford, Connecticut, Police Department (now retired) for his work with the children of that town. *Photo by John Alexopolous, courtesy of The Milford Citizen.*

On duty as a security guard in June of 1985, Chief Big Eagle patrols the City Hall parking lot used by the United Methodist Church in Bridgeport. Ironically, the church is on the corner of Harrison Avenue and Golden Hill Street, the original site of the Golden Hill Reservation. *Photo courtesy of Chief Big Eagle.*

"Rex" greets his master with a kiss. Chief Big Eagle raises shepherds for his work as a security guard. *Photo courtesy of Chief Big Eagle.*

In his spare moments Chief Big Eagle does beadwork on the reservation. Here he displays a beaded belt made for the De Kivas, an Indian advocacy group based in Belgium and the Netherlands. Chief Big Eagle is a foreign correspondent to the *De Kiva Journal* for the eastern North American tribes. Photo by Karin Cooper, courtesy of Chief Big Eagle.

The quarter-acre is not large enough to support the kind of farming once done on the reservation, but Chief Big Eagle tills the soil when he can. The shed in which the Chief lived during construction of the log home has been dated to 1821. Shingles now cover the original plank siding. Storm windows were added by Chief Big Eagle. *Photo courtesy of Chief Big Eagle.*

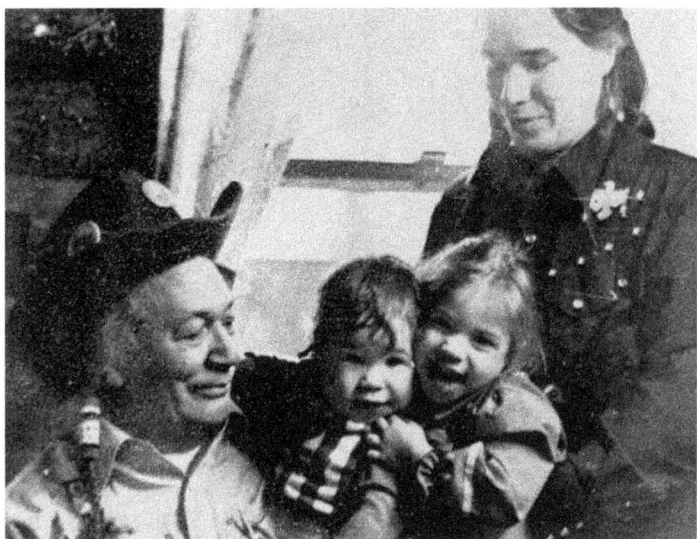

Sharing a happy moment at home are Chief Big Eagle, his son Little Eagle, daughter White Fawn, and wife Marsha. *Photo by Karin Cooper, courtesy of Chief Big Eagle.*

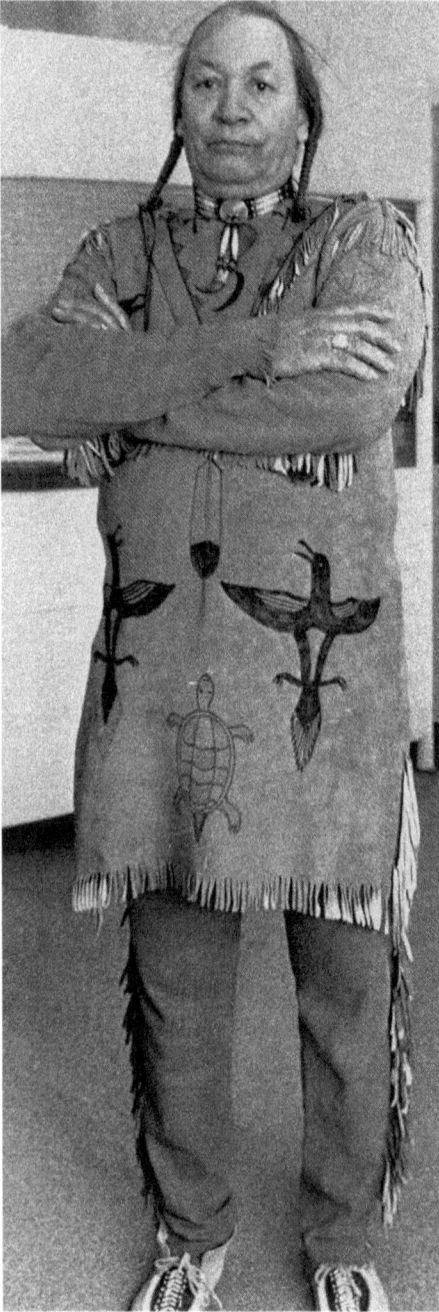

Chief Big Eagle poses in the Department of Environmental Protection while in Hartford for the funeral of Governor Ella Grasso in February of 1981. The Chief attended the funeral at the request of the Governor's family. Following the title search for the quarter-acre, Ella Grasso had personally notified Chief Big Eagle that construction of the log home would resume. *Photo courtesy of Chief Big Eagle.*

PART III

CHAPTER TWENTY-TWO

AFTER THE COURT VICTORY, we thought the war was over. But we were wrong. This was just the beginning.

Not long after Thanksgiving in 1976, the residents and neighbors of Trumbull said that this reservation was not authentic. They demanded proof. They said I wasn't an Indian. They wanted to see the birth certificates of my ancestors. Fortunately, I had already proven these things in order to get on the Connecticut Indian Affairs Council in 1974.

Then the White neighbor who had sued us changed the focus of the fight.

If you stand on the Shelton Road and face this log house, you will see a gravel and oil driveway along the left side of the property. It runs from the edge of the road back toward the shed where I was living while this log house was being built, the shed in which my great-grandfather lived while building the old Sherman homestead. The neighbor had lost the title search for the quarter-acre itself, but he still claimed that the driveway and the shed were his, that they were on his side of the property line.

If the disputed driveway and shed are part of the reservation, then there is enough land for our septic system. There is room for a house and we can live here. But if the driveway and the shed are on the neighbor's property, then there is not enough room for a proper septic system. And we *can't* live here.

The neighbor wanted to tear down the shed and use the driveway as an access road to the woods behind the reservation. He wanted to put in a cul-de-sac back there and develop that valuable property. That is what he wanted to do. But in order to do that, he needed a variance. He had to be able to use the strip of land along the edge of the reservation.

And the funny thing is, when I first returned to the reservation in 1973, I offered the neighbor the driveway. I didn't care about the driveway. I just wanted him to put up a fence to keep the kids out. The neighbor agreed and drew up papers with a lawyer, then changed his mind. I guess he felt at that point that he could get more than just the driveway. That he could get the entire quarter-acre. I don't know. But he could have had the driveway just for the asking.

At the time of the war for this quarter-acre, the White neighbor was a member of the town council. You could see him in the newspaper shouting at the first selectman to get me evicted. And you can read in the newspaper how he put up a garage on the property next door in violation of town codes. The Town of Trumbull initiated action against the neighbor at the request of local residents, who feared the garage was going to be used as rental property. The neighbor was ordered to *cease and desist,* but that garage still stands.

Our White neighbor used the town politicians and the town police. He sent the police out here to the reservation to evict me from the shed. I was living in the shed because the log house was far from complete. And the neighbor said I was trespassing. He said he was going to tear the shed down.

Every day the police would show up with tape measures. They would start at the edge of the Shelton Road and work their way around the property—along the driveway to the shed, then across the back to the woods. They would string out the measuring tapes and roll them back in. They would measure and measure, to see if I was trespassing.

Are you surveyors? I asked them. *What are you measuring? The quarter-acre is one hundred and fourteen feet by one hundred and twenty feet. What are you measuring?*

But they ignored me.

Meanwhile, the White neighbor was getting a permit from the town in order to demolish the shed. He said it was on his property. Therefore it was his. He could tear it down if he wanted to. All he needed was a permit. He said he had paid taxes on the shed in the past. But a state survey done in 1949 showed that the shed was on the quarter-acre. On reservation land.

Many people don't realize that there used to be *another* shed next door, behind the stone house that my grandfather built. But it was torn down because it was filled with rats and snakes. Maybe the neighbor was trying to confuse the two sheds in order to make a claim on reservation land. Maybe he figured it would be easy because at the start there were just two old folks living next door. I don't know. But I don't think he counted on me returning to the quarter-acre.

All this happened in December of 1976, right after our Thanksgiving court victory. I was living in the shed. Other Indians were living in the teepee from time to time. We were waiting for the log house to be built. It was winter. Construction was slow. The house was supposed to be ready in January, but it was nowhere near finished. There was just the foundation, sitting in the snow.

Then the neighbor got his permission to demolish the shed. So Robert Nicola, who had become our lawyer when David Crosby left for the state of Washington, went to court and got an injunction—a court order prohibiting the neighbor from destroying the shed. The judge ordered me to take out $100,000 in liability insurance on the shed, in case something happened.

The shed is assessed by the Town of Trumbull at a value of $60. I paid for the insurance the judge ordered by myself. The neighbor agreed to pay half of it, but I never got my money back.

We were on the reservation and we were ready to fight. Ready for a confrontation. There was a SWAT team based in the Chevron station across the street—Special Weapons and Tactics—like you see on TV. And Clyde Bellecourt said, *Well, here we are. Bring on your jitterbugs and let's get on with it.*

But there was no fight. The lawyers told the police to get off the reservation because the law would not protect them on the reservation. That's one law that is clear. Reservations are Indian country.

But the question of who has criminal jurisdiction over Indian reservations is not clear. According to the state of Connecticut's own researchers, the question of jurisdiction *is as old as the nation and entangled in a complex web of statutes, treaties, and cases.* So they didn't know who had the authority to arrest us if trouble broke out—federal, state, or local officials.

But one thing was clear. Reservations are Indian country. The law would not protect the White Man on Indian property. That is what our lawyers told the police, so the police were disarmed and sent home. Any White Man approaching the reservation was ordered to be put in jail. Because there was nobody here but Indians. And me with my .38 caliber Colt and a 30.06 rifle.

The White neighbor had threatened to bring in a bulldozer and lay the shed flat. And I had said that I would shoot anyone who came on the reservation. It would have been one black day in Trumbull's history. I don't think anyone would have wanted to live in Trumbull after that. Because some of these beautiful homes would have been blown sky high.

But the bulldozer never came. The injunction saw to that. And nobody got hurt. Not that time. Because the police got off the reservation. They stopped trying to evict me from my own property. They stopped their *surveying*. And the bulldozer never came.

The White neighbor was forcing us to fight, so we went back to court. But the Attorney General of the state of Connecticut threw the case wide open. The state did not want to be party to a lawsuit. They didn't want to go to court. And yet the state was supposed to be our trustee.

Massa matchi. Very bad.

CHAPTER TWENTY-THREE

JANUARY CAME. The log house was supposed to be finished in January, but it was far from ready. The winter was cold and the construction was slow.

February came. It was no fun living in the shed all that time. Sometimes I slept in the teepee. Luckily, I did not sleep there on the night of March 3. That night I stayed with a friend in Mansfield. I was going to speak at a school in the morning. My son Kenny was with relatives in Bridgeport.

It was lucky because on the night of March 3, 1977, sometime after 10:00 p.m., the neighbors reported an orange glow in the sky. The teepee was on fire. The fire was reported at 10:40 p.m. The teepee took only six minutes to burn. The teepee that Jane Deerheart let us use was burned to ashes in just six minutes.

The local police and firemen came out to the reservation. And the newspaper reporters. The fire marshal said that the fire had been set. He said it was arson.

And when I returned to the reservation the following afternoon, I was taken into custody and read my rights. Neighbors claimed they had seen me putting wood and propane tanks into the teepee. But my pickup truck was in Mansfield, and I had sold the propane tanks. So you could see it was a set-up.

But no charges were filed. All that was left at the site was a black circle of earth and the charred poles of the teepee, crisscrossed like burnt matchsticks.

Later, our Indian brothers of AIM replaced the teepee with one of their own. And one neighbor claimed she heard a member of AIM say, *If they burn this one, somebody's going to hell.* But talk like that only stirred up trouble. It helped keep the bad feelings alive.

When trouble like this comes to a community, everybody's imagination runs wild. People run off at the mouth. You become a target for all kinds of abuse. Several years later, just when we were trying to bring an end to the legal battles, I was accused of the murders of all those Black children in Atlanta. The charge was made by someone who was only indirectly related to the troubles on the reservation. I never learned about the charge until long after the real murderer was caught. It helped explain why there were so many government agents parked outside, taking pictures of everyone who came to the reservation. Their license plates gave them away. The burning of the teepee brought on a lot of this.

I spoke earlier of the smoke from the wigwams on Golden Hill in Bridgeport. The White Man had burned the wigwams to drive my ancestors from the reservation at the original site. The local officials did nothing about those fires. But the smoke from those flames reached the Creator.

Nothing changes. Several hundred years later a teepee is burned on the reservation again. No arrests are made. Nothing is done about the fire. But the smoke from Jane Deerheart's teepee reached the Creator too. The Creator sees all such smoke.

No matter how much education the White Man gets—he can get a piece of paper and hang it on his wall—his mentality is the same as when he got off the boat three-hundred and fifty years ago. Burn the Indians out and run them off the land.

But I was not about to be burned out or run off, even though things got very tense after the fire. There were arm's length accusations with the neighbors. People shouting and swearing. Bitter words flying back and forth.

And there was fear on both sides. All this noise had been going on for several years, and certain people were deliberately keeping it alive. Other people were getting tired of it. There were threats of physical harm, threats of violence, threats of death. I had put on my gun for my own protection.

The neighbors wanted to drive me off the land and put this land up for sale. They said the Indians were making a mockery of town and state government. But I declared that I would stay on the reservation. No matter what. Because the reservation is sacred land.

CHAPTER TWENTY-FOUR

A MONTH AFTER THE TEEPEE WAS BURNED, there was a big meeting with all parties involved in our case—the Commissioner of the State Department of Environmental Protection, the Indian Affairs Coordinator, representatives from the State Attorney General's office, the First Selectman of the Town of Trumbull, and Indians from the Connecticut Indian Affairs Council. There were representatives from the federal government too—from the United States Department of Justice and the United States Commission on Civil Rights.

I was tired of the harassment and discrimination, and I wanted to see what could be done about all of it. People were trying to evict me from my own property. My neighbor's lawyers wanted all kinds of information about me—where I had lived before, what property I had held, etc.—which my lawyers claimed was *immaterial*. People were writing dirty, filthy letters about me, stuff filled with hate. But when my lawyers tried to get one of those letters from a local press, the press wouldn't give up. It seems everyone had rights except me. If I opened my mouth, I would get sued.

The representatives from the Civil Rights Commission said that the burning of *the teepee indicates lawlessness in the community*. He said that *a firm hand is necessary to protect the Indians on the reservation*.

The harassment and discrimination were one problem we discussed at the meeting. The other was the question of jurisdiction. Who had the power to deal with the case.

As for the harassment, the town selectman said that the problem was just *a neighbor's dispute*. He said that he couldn't be held responsible for the views of his neighbors. But the Indian

Affairs Coordinator said that the problem was larger than that. His office had been receiving phone calls from residents in Trumbull for more than a year and a half. He felt there was a lot of tension in town.

As to the jurisdiction, the representatives from the state Attorney General's office said that the reservation is like a state park. So the state has jurisdiction. But the Indians from the Connecticut Indian Affairs Council said, *No, the reservation is a separate entity.* All the problems came out, but not much was settled. And I told them, *I am not Martin Luther King. You hurt me and somebody's going to get hurt.*

Soon afterward we had a second meeting—just the neighbors, the members of the tribe, and the Indian Affairs Coordinator. The neighbors wanted to know if this is an authentic reservation. And they wanted to know if I have the right to live here. The Indian Affairs Coordinator said that the answer to both questions is *yes.*

People in town know this is a reservation. One of the citizens who works for the town is a relative of one of the families mentioned in William Sherman's diary. In working for the Town of Trumbull, that person signed affidavits years ago stating that this is a reservation.

I had been through all of the questioning before in order to get on the Indian Affairs Council, and I went through it all again. It was a good meeting, but the neighbors weren't satisfied. They were still looking for a way to get rid of me.

So I complained of the threats and harassment to the Connecticut Commission on Human Rights and Opportunities. I told them that people in Trumbull were trying to force me off Indian land. And the Commission wrote back that my *charge does not fall within the jurisdiction* of the Connecticut Public Accommodations Law, 53–36. I was told that the law does not apply to me because I pay no taxes. No rent. They said that *my complaint appears to be a civil matter.* And they suggested I get myself a lawyer.

So I wrote a letter to Richard Blumenthal, the Attorney General of the State of Connecticut, at the Department of Justice. I told him about the court fight with the neighbors, and I told him about the discrimination and harassment. I said that I was being denied my rights as a citizen and that I wanted to bring civil action through a lawsuit. And Mr. Blumenthal wrote back. His letter is downstairs in the museum with all the other documents from this case. Mr. Blumenthal said that his office *could not determine if it has jurisdiction* in cases such as mine. The Department of Justice could not decide who has say over what.

The question of jurisdiction can drive you crazy. At the meeting we had with representatives of the local, state, and federal governments, the Indian Affairs Coordinator spoke of a *shared* or *mixed* jurisdiction. The tribe has jurisdiction on the reservation, the town has criminal jurisdiction, and the state has management jurisdiction. These jurisdictions overlap, but the limits are not clear.

A book called *American Indians and the Law* came out in 1976, right in the middle of the war for this quarter-acre. That book says: *The American Indian occupies a unique position in American society and law. Although United States citizens, reservation Indians are not subject to the Federal Constitution or to the taxes and regulatory controls of the states in which they live and vote.*

American Indians became United States citizens by special legislation in 1924. And, as one of my lawyers says, *therefore presumably possess all the Constitutional rights accorded the rest of our citizens.* Among those is civil rights protection, which is what I wanted. But as my lawyer concluded, *the enforcement of those rights is another matter entirely.*

Jurisdiction is not clear. Indian law is not clear. No one knows what to do in these cases.

CHAPTER TWENTY-FIVE

ON THE SITE OF THE BURNED TEEPEE—between the driveway and the foundation of the log house—there is a fire circle on the reservation today. The fire circle is used in Indian ceremonies. The circle represents the Center of Life. It is made of smooth stones. It is approximately fifteen feet in diameter and is broken by a small opening that faces east. The opening faces the rising sun, the greatest fire.

In the center of the fire circle is a pit of stones, a shallow pit where the sacred fire is kept burning during ceremonies. The medicine man walks around inside the circle and talks to the tribe. The members of the tribe sit in a larger circle outside the stones. The medicine man places tobacco or sweet grass or cedar in the fire as an offering to the Creator. The offering burns, the smoke rises, and the Creator sees it. The Creator sees our ceremonies.

It is the same when the sacred pipe is smoked. The smoke rises to the Creator.

The White Man and the Indians smoked the sacred pipe often. It was smoked when treaties were made. The sacred pipe is like the White Man's Bible. An agreement made with it is sacred. The Indians honored such agreements. The White Man did not. And so blood was shed in the past.

And blood was shed on this reservation. The blood of a White Man, not an Indian.

One evening after the teepee burned, several members of a motorcycle gang came roaring in here on their bikes. I was asleep in the shed. My son Kenny was on patrol. He came in and woke me and said, *Daddy, there's a motorcycle gang out there.* I could tell by the way he said it that he was very scared.

One of the gang members was on foot. He started mouthing off, insulting me. Threatening me. First, he was talking about a stolen motorcycle. Then he claimed it was his gang that had burned the teepee. He said the gang was going to blast us right out of the shed and off the reservation. I told him to shut up and go, but he wouldn't.

I guess everyone around here knew that something was going to happen, because lights went on in all the houses, and heads were hanging out the windows. What happened was that I wasn't going to take any more abuse. When the gang member refused to leave, I shot him with my 30.06 rifle. My lawyers had told me not to shoot, but if it came down to a situation where I had to shoot, to use my rifle, so I could keep the permit for my handgun.

I didn't shoot to kill. Just to make a point. And when I shot, the lights went out all over this neighborhood, and the people disappeared. Then I sent my son to get the police and to give them my rifle.

When the police came, they asked what had happened, and I told them.

Where's the guy? they said.

Crawlin' up the road somewhere, I said.

They went and found him. Then they came back to the reservation. And they said that the guy I had shot had told a different story. That it had all happened differently.

What did you expect him to say? I said.

I thought then that I was done for. That the other members of the motorcycle gang would get me. You don't mess with a motorcycle gang. They come after you.

But I wasn't arrested. No charges were filed. A reservation is Indian country. And I guess the gang figured that it was just between me and that one guy. We made a truce, and nothing else happened.

The wonder is that I didn't start shooting a lot earlier. *Years* earlier. The wonder is that we didn't hole up in the frozen foundation of the log house and blast away at everybody—police, neighbors, firemen, SWAT team. Because we were mad. We had a right to be mad. We had been mad for over three hundred years.

But only one shot was fired in the war for this quarter-acre. I fired it myself. And the smoke from my 30.06 rifle rose into the sky. The Creator saw it. The Creator saw it just as He had seen the smoke from the burning wigwams on Golden Hill years ago. And the smoke from the burning teepee.

The Creator saw the smoke from my rifle. And He will deal with me in His own way.

CHAPTER TWENTY-SIX

IN THE SPRING OF 1977, the Third Annual Native American Day was held in Westport. Indians came from all over Connecticut to gather for ceremonies and celebrations. White people came too. There were many speakers, and one topic common to all was the fight of the Golden Hill people against the reservation neighbors in Trumbull.

The case was far from settled. As one newspaper reporter said, I had gone *on the law path.* There was no more violence. We wanted to settle things peacefully in court.

One of the speakers at the Native American Day was Thomas Tureen, a lawyer for the Native American Rights Fund. Using the 1790 Non-Intercourse Act I mentioned earlier, Mr. Tureen had helped Indians lay claim to half the state of Maine. In regard to the case of the Golden Hill People, he said, *We are testing not only the strength of this nation's promises to Indian people, we are testing the strength of this nation's promises, period. The strength of the nation's legal system. And we are going to find out how much that legal system is worth.*

Mr. Tureen concluded by saying that the staff members of NARF would be available to help us in the present court fight over the reservation boundary—the fight for the driveway and shed.

Another speaker was Alvin Josephy. He has written several books about Native Americans. He said that there is very little understanding of the present generation of Indian people. He said that White people are asking, *What do these Indians really want and why are they so hostile toward us?*

He spoke of a *White backlash.* White people are getting angry because Indians are speaking up and making progress in controlling their own affairs. He called on the present generation of White Americans to *break the long chain of deceit*. He called on them to be honest and fair in their treatment of Indians.

Indians feel this backlash is due to ignorance, because the schools do not teach anything about Indians today. Local non-Indian groups around the country have even formed an organization—the Interstate Congress for Equal Rights—to fight against the Indian gains. And a report from the United States Commission on Civil Rights shows that tribal victories of the 1970s *have been eclipsed* by the reaction of non-Indians against the tribes.

But as Senator Hatfield said at a hearing in 1977, *We have found a very significant backlash that by any other name comes out as racism in all its ugly manifestations.*

The annual Native American Day is not just for Indians. It is to show other people what Indian life is all about. It is a good day for both Indians and non-Indians. It is an event that is held each year. You can watch for it and attend.

A month after the Third Annual Native American Day, I received a letter from the Indian Affairs Coordinator saying that the log house was ready and officially available for occupation. So at the end of June, we had a grand housewarming. It was organized by the Connecticut Friends of Indians, Incorporated. More than two hundred people attended, both Indians and Whites.

As with the Native American Day, there were ceremonies and celebrations. Indians came dressed in their full regalia. Hair was tied back with mink skin. I wore my ceremonial ghost-dance shirt. It is a buckskin shirt marked with a waterbird and the insignia of my clan—the Bear Clan. My feathered medicine stick and pipe were hung on the wall.

There was drumming and dancing and singing. Indians did the rabbit dance and the deer dance and the Sioux ghost dance. And Indians sang the anthem of AIM. There was sweet grass for the ceremonial fires and there was Indian food too, like watercress salad, green bean casserole, batter-dipped greens, and codfish. We opened the museum in the basement of the log house. There was a slide show—slides of the Golden Hill Tribe, our lineage, and our heritage.

And there were speakers. William Alpert, a scholar who studies

Indian life, told the history of the Paugussett people, how our ancestors lived, how they traveled. He told about our Algonquian language, using simple examples. The word *waug*, he said, means *place*. So the Wepawaugs, one of the five tribes of the Paugussett confederacy, lived in the place of the reservoir or river, the *wepa*, in Milford.

Mr. Alpert talked about the Indian families or clans. He said, *Only the Clan Mother can de-horn the chief.* Only the Clan Mother can take the deer horns from the chief's gustoweha and say that he is no longer chief.

The White people at the housewarming learned a lot about Indians from Mr. Alpert. I have his talk on tape. We play it for people who visit the museum. And he concluded, *There is not much life for an Indian in Connecticut today.*

But it was a happy day for us. More than two years after the old Sherman homestead had been demolished, the log house was finally ready. I moved in with my family. And my ancestors moved in too.

CHAPTER TWENTY-SEVEN

IN TELLING THIS STORY I am not using many names. Since I returned to the reservation in the summer of 1973, the state of Connecticut has had three different governors. The attorney general has changed too. And the Coordinator of Indian Affairs. Their names do not matter. They are always White, never Indian. And whenever you write them, you get an answer from someone else.

Couldn't an Indian be of use in the government? Indians would make good game wardens, good conservation officers. Who knows the land better than an Indian? But you do not find any Indians in government.

And the names of the neighbors do not matter. They are always White. And there is always someone who wants to take Indian land. Fortunately, there are neighbors who will support you too.

But the federal government has not been very helpful. When you need them, the laws don't apply. Or they can't decide if they have jurisdiction. And the state government is supposed to be your trustee, but they don't want to get involved. They don't want to be party to a lawsuit. They don't care if your tribe is legally terminated, and they give you a council with no real power. And when the neighbors try to run you off your land, the local police come out like surveyors and measure your property.

No help from the feds, no help from the state, no help from the local officials. It was the same for my ancestors. Even your own Indian brothers won't support you. Except for AIM. Everywhere you look, there is no help. And when that happens, there is nothing to do but take your gun and stand your ground.

And yet, through stubbornness and determination, the Golden

Hill people have been able to get some help, because there are agencies like Housing and Urban Development (HUD) and the Comprehensive Employment and Training Act (CETA) that will aid Indians whether or not they are federally recognized. But it is never easy. Let me give you a few examples.

When I moved into this log house with my family, the legal war for the quarter-acre was not over. We were still fighting over the reservation boundary, over who owned the driveway and the shed. The house had been built with a holding tank, which has to be pumped each month, because my neighbor claimed there was not enough room for a proper septic system.

We soon learned just how small this quarter-acre is. There was no room for the tribe to gather. So we applied to HUD for money to buy more land. We set up the Golden Hill Development Corporation, just like White men do, to help ourselves become self-sufficient as a tribe.

And in 1979 we received a grant of $69,000 from HUD. With that money we bought sixty-nine acres of land in Colchester, Connecticut. Colchester is to the northeast of here, about in the middle of the state. Later we got a second grant and expanded those sixty-nine acres to one hundred and eight. But let me tell you what happens when an Indian goes out to buy land. Suddenly there is no land for sale.

There were seventy acres for sale in Waterbury, on a mountain top. I liked the land very much. But when the people heard that Indians were going to buy the land for a reservation, they raised so much hell I said to forget it.

The people complained that Indians were getting money from the federal government while they were getting nothing. They never stopped to think of all the factories, and farmers, and people living in rural areas who get their homes with money from the Federal Housing Authority. Cities and towns get money from HUD too. Just like we did.

But we didn't buy the land in Waterbury because I figured that if we were going to fight even before we got there, we'd be fighting all along.

Next, we found one hundred and twenty-one acres of land for sale in Stafford Springs. It was beautiful land, and we offered the owner $69,000 for it. But he turned around and sold it to a developer for $50,000. We could have taken him to court because of the real estate laws, but that would have meant another fight. And we were tired of fighting.

So we looked around some more and found the land in Colchester. This time we had a man from the federal government contact the real estate agent. Only the government man didn't identify himself. I went along with him to see the land. But the agent stopped the car at the edge of town and said that when it came to minorities, he usually didn't go any farther because they would never get the money for the property. The loans always fell through.

So the government man identified himself and suddenly there was plenty of land for sale.

Later, the real estate agent said, *Well, I don't think the owner wants to let this land go for only $69,000.* And the government man said, *You made a deal.*

So we bought the land. We only had a certain amount of time in which to spend the money. But the main reason I took the land in Colchester was that when the people heard that Indians were buying the land for a reservation, they said they would welcome us, that they had nothing against Indians. And they have been very good to us. There have been no problems, no complaints.

But I would much rather have had the land in Waterbury, those seventy acres on the top of the mountain. The land in Colchester is wetland—wooded, wet, and flat. It is definitely not prime land. My son is in charge of the land in Colchester today. There is a cabin there, a trailer, some horses, and some *wickiups* or wigwams. But it will take a long time before that land is developed. It's going to take money.

We have applied for funds under CETA to help young Indians develop worthwhile skills so Indians can be independent and have economic control over their own lives. But when the money comes from the government, there are always strings attached. We used to receive revenue-sharing funds, just like other towns do, but I stopped that, because the government is always telling you what to do and how to live. That's the problem with Big Brother and Big Business.

But I still dream of the day when the more than one hundred members of the Golden Hill tribe of the Paugussett Indian nation can live together on the land in Colchester. When we can get back to the land and make things happen.

CHAPTER TWENTY-EIGHT

DOWNSTAIRS IN THE TRIBAL MUSEUM is a library of Indian materials. The shelves go from the floor to the ceiling. Many of the books are reports from the federal government, *findings and recommendations* of various *task forces* and *committees* dealing with Indian problems. The reports are as thick as the White Man's Bible. They come out every year.

Here are some of the titles: *Federal Administration and Structure of Indian Affairs; Federal Indian Law Consolidation, Revision and Codification; Federal, State, and Tribal Jurisdiction; Terminated and Non-Federally Recognized Indians; Indian Health; Religious Discrimination: A Neglected Issue; Jurisdiction on Indian Reservations; Indian Education; Alcohol and Drug Abuse; Oil and Gas Leases on Indian Land; Federal Programs of Assistance to American Indians; Steelhead Trout Protection; Indian Tribes: A Continuing Quest for Survival.*

Native Americans are the most written about and legislated minority in the United States, given our small number of less than one million. Each year the government comes out with thousands of pages of reports. If you read these reports—and any good library will have them—you will find that the government admits that it has not been very helpful to Indians.

The same statements appear over and over: *Inaction and missed opportunities characterize the seeming inability of the United States to implement effectively the promises and commitments it has historically made to the tribes. The present system for protecting Indian rights has significant limitations—coherent mechanisms for determining and implementing Indian policy are lacking; and conflicts over Indian rights exacerbate pre-existing problems Indians face concerning denials of equal protection of the law.*

If this society through its government does not live up to its promises and commitments to Indian people, then no rights are secure. The reports speak of the *long history of the best treatment of Indians being that of neglect.*

Take the problem of federal recognition. The Bureau of Indian Affairs has no services for terminated tribes or tribes that are not federally recognized, which means most of the eastern tribes. This includes the Golden Hill people of the Paugussett nation. And the government isn't even sure what it means by an *Indian.* According to one report, *The application of imprecise terminology and varying definition of "Indian" on all levels of government has led to confusion about the status of terminated and non-federally recognized Indians and the responsibilities of the federal government to such Indians.* Is that what George Washington meant by *fatherly care?*

I have a folder in the filing cabinet downstairs dealing with our ongoing attempt to gain federal recognition for the Golden Hill tribe. One of the things the government requires for a tribe to be recognized is that you have your ceremonies. But the neighbors complain about our ceremonies.

In June of 1977, not long after the housewarming, we had a wake on the reservation for a young Navajo who was electrocuted on his job. He was one of the Indians who helped us set up the teepee that was burned. His parents requested that he lie in state in a traditional way. You can't do that at a funeral home because there is more than one body on view at a time. So we had a wake here at the reservation, and I spoke at the ceremony.

But the neighbors complained that the Indian was not a member of the immediate family. They complained about *disruptive traffic* and *loud and boisterous* noise. You can't win. You try to please the federal government and you upset your neighbors.

Here are some more statements from those reports in the museum library:

The dominant society has generally characterized Indians with stylized romanticism or blatant stereotypes, and "different" and "separate" all too often have translated as "inferior" and "unequal." Another factor prevalent throughout the history of the United States and Indian relations has been economic greed. Indians have possessed land and other resources that non-Indians wanted. Non-Indians have usually prevailed . . . One of the greatest

141

obstacles faced by the Indian today in his drive for self-determination and a place in this nation is the American public's ignorance of the historical relation of the United States with Indian tribes and the lack of general awareness of the status of an Indian in our society today.

I don't need these reports to tell me these things. I have seen them every day of my life.

Based on past treaties and federal laws, the Indian tribes of today exist as *separate political entities* with special rights. The Constitution of the United States gives Congress *plenary power*— full and complete power—over Indian affairs. The title to Indian land and resources is either held in trust by the federal government or is held by the tribes themselves. Tribes have their own *domestic powers,* and the states have *no inherent powers* on the reservations. Many of the tribes today have their own constitutions, but these are not recognized by the federal government.

And even though this special status exists for Indians, the reports will tell you that *no consistent standard of responsibility has been established to define and delimit the plenary power of Congress over the entire range of Indian affairs.*

Things got so confusing a few years back that Congress chartered a special commission—the American Indian Policy Review Committee—to study the Indian situation. In 1976, right in the middle of the war for this quarter-acre, that committee concluded, among other things, that *only the Indian people themselves can tell the real story.*

And that is what I am doing.

CHAPTER TWENTY-NINE

IN 1978, ANOTHER COMMISSION WAS FORMED—the Commission on State-Tribal Relations. It was the first nationally organized attempt to get the tribes and states working together without threatening the jurisdiction of either side. There had been nothing but tension and hostility and suspicion between the states and the tribes in the 1970s because of the many lawsuits, like the kind we were going through in the fight for this quarter-acre.

The reports from this particular commission admit that the courts and Congress *generate significant blocks* to good relations between the tribes and the states. The commission was formed to help the Indian leaders and the state officials *negotiate their own solutions* to their problems.

As far as I can see, that is the latest direction in Indian affairs. The federal government wants the states to work things out with their tribes through *agreements and/or compacts*. I mention this now because you are probably wondering how the legal war for this quarter-acre ended. Let me tell you about the *solution*.

A deal was made. The court fighting continued until 1982. And then a deal was made. The surveys showed that the shed and the driveway were on reservation property, as we had said all along. The tribe was declared to be the *absolute owner* of the property here, but the neighbor who had been after us got an *easement* on the driveway—he got the right to use the driveway—from the Superior Court of Fairfield at Bridgeport.

The White neighbor who had been after us never lived next door during the war. He has always rented out the stone house there, the house that my grandfather built. He is developing the land behind the reservation, and his renters can use our driveway.

A deal was made. The state bought the disputed land and allowed the neighbor to use it. The neighbor received several thousand dollars, plus half of what he had paid in survey fees. And he never paid me for the insurance on the shed.

The deal was made in the Attorney General's office, not at the table where we had all met to agree to terms. The neighbor never showed up at a meeting we had to sign what the Indian lawyers had drawn up. His own papers were signed by the Attorney General and our lawyers never saw them.

The state of Connecticut and the White neighbor drink out of the same glass. How can an Indian break that glass?

That was the *solution*. The state bought the land along the edge of the reservation and allowed the neighbor to use it. But it didn't end the war.

In the winter of 1984, our lawyers had the case reopened, to get the land that includes the driveway and the shed put in the name of the tribe with the rest of the quarter-acre. Because by state law, the state cannot own Indian land. And at the same time we reopened the case, we made a request for a fence and a proper septic system, to get rid of the holding tank.

But the Attorney General didn't want to go to court. It costs too much money. And if the judge asked the state to sign the land over to the tribe, the state would have to appeal, because the state has *sovereign immunity*. It cannot be sued.

So a bill was introduced into the legislature to give the commissioner of the state Department of Environmental Protection the power to sign over land that the state of Connecticut has no interest in. Then the entire title of this quarter-acre reservation would be signed over to the Golden Hill tribe—the title to the reservation plus the strip of land along the boundary—and that would be an end of it. No one would ever again be able to make a claim against us.

But let me tell you what happened with that legislation. The bill read as follows: *The Commissioner... shall convey by quitclaim deed to the Golden Hill Paugussett Tribe whatever interest the state of Connecticut may have in the Golden Hill Paugussett Reservation in Trumbull, Connecticut . . . the land shall remain under the care and management of the Department of Environmental Protection.* The bill was attached to another piece of legislation, but when my lawyer from the Connecticut Indian Law Project went to check out the bill, she couldn't find it. It had been attached to a different piece of legislation from what she had been told. The new bill dealt with a similar transfer of land in the town of Enfield. But we were never told of the switch.

And when my lawyer finally located the bill, this is what we found. A new clause had been added at the very end, so the bill now read that the land would remain under the care and management of the Department of Environmental Protection *until a conveyance is made in accordance with the provision of this section.* What that means is that once the land was transferred to the tribe, the state would no longer have anything to do with us. Services to the reservation would end. The tribe would be terminated.

My lawyer didn't believe me, but I raised such a fuss when she showed me the bill that we went to the Attorney General. The Attorney General claimed to know nothing of the provision. He *suspected the legislative commissioner's office added it without any knowledge of Indian law.*

He admitted, however, that the commissioner of the Department of Environmental Protection had agreed to maintain services after the transfer of land. But he said it was too late to amend the bill. He told us to wait until next session. But we told him it was unacceptable to wait.

Waiting would have meant more legal battles a year later.

So we contacted the Department of Environmental Protection's liaison who, in the words of my lawyer, was *visibly embarrassed* at the *apparent mistake.* He agreed to push for an amendment, the amendment went through, and the bill was passed, signed by the governor in May of 1984.

But had I slept on this, we'd have been gone. The town of Trumbull would have been able to tax the land. We wouldn't have been able to afford to stay here. The reservation would have come to an end. But the governor signed the bill, and the case is closed.

In a letter to the lawyer who had reopened our case, my lawyer from the Connecticut Indian Law Project said that the provision of the bill, until we got it amended, had been *THE OPPOSITE* of what we had been told. The capital letters are hers. In her analysis of what happened, she wrote: *It is unclear whether the Attorney General or the Department of Environmental Protection intentionally agreed to the provision which would have ended services to the reservation. However, the failure of the Attorney General to check the language and to inform us of the addition could have caused serious consequences, especially because the Attorney General had expressed his opinion that the entire Connecticut Indian Affairs Council should be abolished.*

As she said, *it would not be inconsistent for him to end services to the reservation.* But the governor signed the bill, and the case is closed.

When I returned to the reservation in 1973, people in the state were trying to terminate the Golden Hill tribe. Today, with the very legislation that was supposed to have ended the matter once and for all, people in the state are still trying to do the same thing.

It is no different from what happened to my ancestors more than three hundred years ago.

CHAPTER THIRTY

SO THE WAR FOR THIS QUARTER-ACRE IS OVER. That heartache, at least, is in the past. But the heartache continues, because an invisible war is being fought every day—by the Golden Hill tribe and Indians all over America. The war is being fought because Indians still have many grievances.

Indians want their tribes to be recognized. Indians want terminated tribes to be returned to tribal status. Indians want sacred tribal lands returned. Indians want to end archaeological digs that disturb our burial grounds because it is disrespectful and sacrilegious to treat human remains as museum exhibits.

Indians want mission churches removed from the reservations because we have our own church—the Native American Church. Indians want the Environmental Protection Agency to become a separate department of the United States government, so that economic programs can be developed and reservation resources can be properly maintained. And Indians want an Indian university.

The invisible war continues because, when people think of Indians, they still think of John Wayne and his Comancheros on TV. They think of Indians in war bonnets. But only the Plains Indians wear bonnets. You'd look like a fool running through the woods with a bonnet on your head.

Not all Indians wear bonnets or wear their hair the same way. The Hopi wear their hair to the side. The Apache wear their hair shoulder length. The Navajo wear their hair in a bun. Only the Plains Indians wear bonnets full of feathers.

Such misconceptions continue the invisible war. People still think that western Indians are western Indians. But most of the western Indians were originally from the east—the Creek, the Chickasaw, the Pawnee, the Sioux, the Cherokee—all of those tribes were originally from the east.

Years ago, when the Paugussett nation broke up, many of our people joined the Iroquois in New York. It was the Iroquois who ran the Sioux out of New York. The Huron ran them farther, and the United States Army ran them out of Minnesota to the Plains. That's how the Sioux went west.

Or take the Cherokee. In 1838 President Andrew Jackson used the Army to enforce an illegal treaty that required the Cherokee to move out of Tennessee. They were driven all the way to Oklahoma. Four thousand Indians died on that march. It was known as The Trail of Tears. Some of the Cherokee hid out in the Smoky Mountains and stayed in the east. Only recently, in the spring of 1984, have they had a council with their brothers in the west, as they try to reunite their divided nation. Reservations for many of these eastern tribes were set up out west in the 1800s, after the Constitution of the United States came into being. But the Golden Hill Reservation was set up in 1659, not long after the White Man came to America.

The invisible war continues each time an Indian child is born. Let me give you an example.

I have eighteen children. And many grandchildren. I have been married four times. It is difficult for a woman to marry an Indian chief because she marries his tribe. She marries his ancestors and his responsibilities.

My youngest child is a boy. His name is I-Hahm-Tet. It means Little Eagle. His name is Little Eagle because I am Big Eagle. Little Eagle was born in 1983. And when he was born, the woman at the hospital put his name on the birth certificate in this manner: First name, Little; middle name, Eagle. And my wife told this woman, *His name is Little Eagle. No middle name.*

But it doesn't fit the form, the woman said.

Indians never fit the form, because the form is made by a White Man.

So I went to the hospital administrator and asked if the birth certificate shouldn't be changed. *I suppose so,* she said. So the record was changed at the hospital, but not at the Bureau of Vital Statistics in Bridgeport. The hospital would not send a corrected form to the Bureau of Vital Statistics.

So I went to the Bureau of Vital Statistics, and the person there promptly crossed out Little Eagle's middle name and wrote in *at request of father.* That puts the blame on me.

But I made no mistake.

And let me tell you why this is so important. There was a man at the hospital who had worked on the land claims of the Native Alaskans. He said, *Any birth certificate with any mark on it does not go. It's invalid.*

I know of a Schaghticoke Indian who was refused her Indian status here in Connecticut because someone had written *Schaghticoke Tribe* on her birth certificate. So it was not a valid document.

So my son Little Eagle has two strikes against him already in his life. First, he's an Indian. Second, his birth certificate has been tampered with. *At request of father.*

And yet changes *are* made on birth certificates. When a woman has a baby and doesn't know who the father is, she can come in a year or two later and add the father's name. So why can't changes be made for Indians? Why are there two standards?

My youngest daughter lives here on the reservation. She is three years old. Her name is Waup Athoo Kwey. It means White Fawn. Her first name is not White. Her middle name is not Fawn. Her name is Waup Athoo Kwey. White Fawn.

The invisible war continues wherever the schools do not teach the truth. I'm sure that most people around here—despite all the noise of the war for this quarter-acre—aren't even aware that this is an Indian reservation. Because schools don't teach anything about local Indians. They don't know much about local Indians. That is why I have agreed to tell my story.

It is in the greatest interests of history that the truth be told, that we teach the truth. So that future generations will walk in truth.

So the heartache continues, but things have quieted down around here at the reservation in Trumbull. The neighbors have quieted down, because we have had our *day in court.* And one of the neighbors responsible for keeping alive a lot of the noise during the war no longer lives across the street. She was evicted from the house she was renting. With her five children.

This was a woman who liked to think of herself as *the great Indian fighter of Trumbull*. She fought hard to get me evicted from this reservation. And what happened? *She* was the one who got evicted. It happened just before Thanksgiving in 1983. You can see the photo in *The Bridgeport Post*. She had trouble making her rent.

But I hold no grudge against this woman, because I feel she was used by others who wanted to run the Indians out of town. She was encouraged to keep up the noise—the lies and the accusations. But the Creator doesn't like that kind of ugliness. And so, just before Thanksgiving, she was evicted. And the Indians are still here.

Forever.

CHAPTER THIRTY-ONE

INDIGENOUS MEANS *NATIVE.* Indigenous people are native people, the original inhabitants of a particular place. The term is usually applied to people of primitive cultures. When White Americans think of *natives,* they often think of tribes in Africa or the Amazon jungle. But America has its own native people—the American Indians.

The natives of America were but one group represented at an international conference in Geneva, Switzerland, in 1981, when one hundred and thirty representatives of indigenous peoples came together from all over the globe, from every continent except Antarctica. The purpose of the conference was to call international attention to the desperate conditions in which the indigenous peoples of today are struggling to survive.

A report of that conference from the United Nations' offices says that *the root of the problem is the denial of the right of indigenous people to their land.* The conference blamed international corporations which, in search of profits, grab the land of indigenous people, deny these people the right to self-determination, and destroy their traditional way of life.

The conference also warned about the consequences of a nuclear arms race, its effect upon the life and the land of indigenous peoples. The representatives asked that the question of indigenous people be on the agenda of a United Nations conference in 1983. And they asked that a work group be formed, with the power to gather information, hear testimony of indigenous people, and investigate the most urgent situations worldwide.

I mention this international movement because the Golden Hill people are a part of it.

In the years since the reservation housewarming, since the museum in the basement has been open, this quarter-acre has been visited by many people. I have a guest book that the visitors sign. It has been signed by people from all over the world. It has been signed by Arab sheiks that came from the Middle East to see the *first* Americans. The Native Americans.

And the guest book has been signed by scholars from the Netherlands. Every summer these scholars come from Europe to the reservation. They are tracing the Dutch traders who came to America in the days of my ancestors. They want to learn how their countrymen affected American life. The man in charge of these scholars is Franz Wojciechowski. He is writing a book in the Dutch language and it will include the story of the Golden Hill people of the Paugussett Indian nation.

It would be good if more American scholars showed the same interest in writing the truth about early life in America, when my ancestors first lost their land.

I have been working with another foreign group, too—the De Kivas. I am the foreign correspondent of the Eastern North American tribes to the *De Kiva Journal*.

The De Kivas are based in Belgium and the Netherlands. They are a work group that takes the Indian cases before the International Human Rights Council in Geneva, Switzerland. They have tried to make an international case out of the 1868 Fort Laramie Treaty, which the Sioux made with the United States government. The Sioux allowed the American people to put roads across their reservation lands out west in the 1800s. But the treaty was largely a trick, and the Sioux ended up fighting for, and losing, their land.

The De Kivas work for justice in such cases. As a gift, I have made a beaded belt for the De Kivas. It has a buffalo head in the center. When I have time, I do beadwork downstairs in the museum. Such belts are used for decoration today, but in the past they were used for ceremonies and treaties as well. So you can see there is a lot of international interest in this tiny quarter-acre. I hope such interest will help put an end to the invisible war.

You can help too. By knowing the truth. By speaking the truth. You can come out to the reservation. See the museum. Hear the tapes of the scholars. You can see what a traditional log house is like.

I am retired now, and I am usually here at the reservation. We are across the street from the Chevron station on the Shelton Road. I am usually here, except for the first and third Tuesday of each month. On those days I work with inmates at a prison in Somers, Connecticut. I am a founding member and counselor of the Native American Prison Project. I visit the Native American inmates and help them with their spiritual needs. I bring in the sacred drum and the sacred pipe and explain our history. Non-Indians attend these sessions too, and they have been as appreciative as the Indians themselves.

I have worked with prisoners at the state correctional unit at Huntingdon, Pennsylvania, and in the federal penitentiary at Lewisburg, Pennsylvania too. Closer to home, I have worked with the Greater Bridgeport Area Council on Alcoholism. I have been a consultant and instructor in the Indian education program for the Bridgeport elementary schools, a program I started myself. And I have been a member of the Minority Advisory Council of the Department of Aging.

All these things keep me busy in retirement. The work is very necessary. But if you try, you can find me here at the reservation.

So come out for a visit. When I see you, I will say *Saygo*, which means *Greetings in Good Health*. And when you leave, I will say *Onenh*, which means *'Til our paths cross again*.

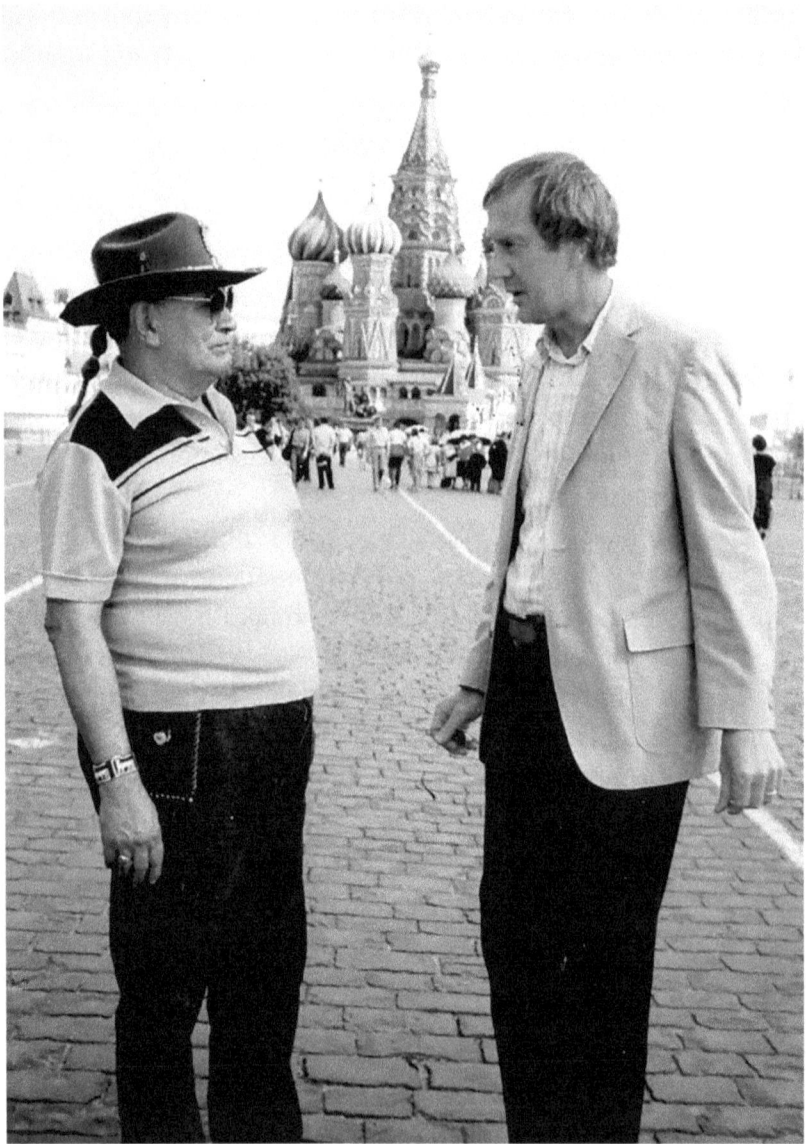

Chief Big Eagle and Claude Clayton Smith traveled to Moscow in the summers of 1990 and 1991 at the invitation of Dr. Alexander Vashchenko, of the Gorky Institute of World Literature, who translated *Quarter-Are of Heartache* into Russian. Their experiences resulted in Smith's book *Red Men in Red Square* (Pocahontas Press, 1994).

AFTERWORD

SUBSEQUENT TO THE LEGISLATIVE VICTORY of the Golden Hill Tribe in the spring of 1984, developments elsewhere threatened to change the complexion of Indian rights in the state of Connecticut.

Senator Lowell Weicker, acting on a request by the Board of Selectmen of the Town of North Stonington, conducted an investigation into the question of jurisdiction on the state's Indian reservations. The action was initiated following a dispute between rival factions of the Eastern Pequot tribe.

Discussing the problem with the United States Attorney and the state's attorney, Senator Lowell Weicker decided that the state has criminal jurisdiction over the Indian reservations, and he arranged for the state police to monitor any criminal action between the disputing Pequot factions on their reservation site. The State of Connecticut stood behind the Senator.

Kenneth Piper, Chief Big Eagle's son, now in his twenties and in charge of the Golden Hill Reservation in Colchester, Connecticut, led a demonstration of Indians from all over New England to protest the state's decision. The tribes gathered at the Golden Hill Reservation to pray and perform native dances, hoping to convince the state that the Indians plan to resist interference by state police.

"Everything that the Indians have fought for in the 1950s, the 1960s, and especially in the 1970s," the Chief's son told one reporter, "is being taken away from us by this." He argued that Indians had earned the right to self-determination and should be "allowed to carry on as a sovereign nation."

Thus the question of jurisdiction has been reopened with a

new intensity, and the Indian tribes of Connecticut continue to squabble among themselves as they did over three hundred years ago, while trying to unite in the face of the White Man's rule.

Shawsville, Virginia
December 1984

TODAY, CONNECTICUT'S JURISDICTION over its Indian reservations involves a complex interplay of state authority and tribal sovereignty, varying among the state's federally recognized tribes. The petition of the Golden Hill Paugussett Indians for federal recognition was denied in 1996 and again in 2004. Officials at the Bureau of Indian Affairs in Washington, D.C. argued that the tribe is restricted to members of the Sherman family. Other tribal members were scattered across the United States in the diaspora following the repeated relocation of the 1659 reservation in Bridgeport. In 2017 tribal lawyers challenged the "no second chance rule" that prevents tribes previously denied recognition from repetitioning. As of August 2024, reports indicate that the Golden Hill Paugussetts, along with the Schaghticoke and Eastern Pequot tribes, may have a new opportunity to pursue federal recognition. The current status of this possibility, however, remains unclear.

Madison, Wisconsin
April 2025

PAUGUSSETT TRIBAL
CHIEF BIG EAGLE
1916-2008

Connecticut Post
Tuesday, August 5, 2008

Recognition fight was chief's legacy

By PETER URBAN
Staff writer

As he lay in a teepee in the woods outside Leningrad, Aurelius Piper felt a horrifying pain in his chest and thought he was about to die.

Piper, known to the 150 Russian Indianists gathered at the 1991 powwow as Chief Big Eagle, woke Irina Loukina and, in his gravely ill voice, told her he needed to climb to the top of a nearby hill.

"If I'm going to die. I'm going to die up there," he said.

They reached the top and there performed a blood ceremony where she became his adopted Indian daughter. Others in the group performed their own ritual ceremony — offering up a bit of themselves so the chief would live.

Paugussett tribal chief dies at 91

Continued from **A1**

Claude Clayton Smith's voice cracked Monday as he retold the story, having learned only hours before that the hereditary chief of the Golden Hill Paugussett Indian Tribe had died Sunday morning of natural causes on the tribe's reservation in Trumbull. He was 91.

"I didn't think he would ever die," Smith said. "He was such a tough guy, mentally and physically. His mother lived to be 104 years old."

Piper, born Aug. 30, 1916, was named chief in 1959 by his mother, Chieftess Rising Star, and battled afterward to preserve the quarter-acre state reservation in Trumbull that is surrounded by suburban homes.

He later secured a federal grant that allowed the tribe to purchase land in Colchester, where the tribe established a second, 106-acre state reservation. Piper also fought unsuccessfully for federal recognition as a way to preserve his culture and heritage — a battle that began before there were any thoughts of casino riches.

The tribe sent a letter of intent to the Department of the Interior in 1982 saying that it planned to petition for recognition. The Bureau of Indian Affairs ultimately rejected the request in 2004 saying that the tribe failed to meet the criteria necessary for approval.

During the fight for recognition, the Paugussetts filed claims to more than 700,000 acres of land, setting off a flurry of legal challenges that ended in 1998 when the state Supreme Court refused to hear their appeal. The land claims, which stretched from Middletown to Wilton, and from Greenwich through lower Westchester County, N.Y., were eventually dropped, but could have been revived if the tribe won federal recognition.

In 1993, Piper's son, Kenneth, also known

as Moonface Bear, was a key figure in a 10-week standoff between State Police and the Colchester faction of the tribe for selling untaxed cigarettes on its reservation. Piper and his son, Aurelius Piper Jr., known as Council Chief Quiet Hawk, had opposed the cigarette sales and banished Moonface Bear from the tribe. Kenneth Piper died in 1996.

Michael O'Connell, a Hartford attorney who represents the tribe, said Monday that during the 1990s Piper had begun to step back from the political operations of the tribe, leaving that responsibility to his sons.

"It was time for the next generation to step to the forefront," O'Connell said. "He stepped to the background but his personality was clearly conveyed. He was a fascinating figure who had strong feelings and a clear devotion to his heritage and to those still active in the tribe."

Richard Velky, chief of the Schaghticoke Tribe, which has an office in Derby, said Monday that he had known Piper since the 1970s when Piper was active in forming the Connecticut Indian Affairs Council.

"He was strong for his people and his leadership will be missed by all of us," Velky said. "He was great to sit down and have a conversation with. He was a well-respected individual — certainly in my book."

In the 1990s, Piper began to spend more time in Springfield, Maine, where he eventually lived full time raising deer.

Smith, who grew up in Stratford, met Piper in the early 1980s after his parents sent him a newspaper article about the chief.

Smith, who was teaching at Virginia Tech, was nearing completion of a novel, "The Stratford Devil," which mentioned the Paugussett tribe. He visited Piper at his log cabin home in Trumbull and became enthralled with Piper's struggle to keep his home. They collaborated on a book "Quarter-

Acre of Heartache" that told the story.

"Quarter-Acre of Heartache" was published in 1985. Smith, now a writer in residence at Illinois College, was with Piper when he suffered the heart attack near Leningrad.

The two traveled to Russia in 1990 and 1991 at the invitation of Alexander Vaschenko, a Russian authority on American Indian literature. Smith had given a copy of "Quarter-Acre of Heartache" to Vaschenko.

On the second trip, Piper and Smith participated in the powwow where about 150 Indian enthusiasts gathered to celebrate American Indian heritage.

The Russians attending the powwow had been engrossed by American Indians since Soviet propagandists first began focusing on them as an exploited minority of American capitalism in the 1970s.

The chief met Loukina on his first visit to Russia and they solidified their family bond on the second trip. He helped her emigrate to the U.S. She earned a master's degree at the University of Toledo. She now lives in Maine.

"She talked on the phone with the chief on Saturday. In a whisper he told her 'come and get me.' He died Sunday," Smith said.

Smith wrote the book "Red Men in Red Square" about Piper's trips to Russia. "He really made that powwow in 1991," Smith said.

Piper served on many boards and commissions throughout Connecticut, fighting for the rights of American Indians and other minority groups.

He also served in the U.S. military during World War II, according to the tribe.

He is survived by his wife, Marsha Conte Piper, five children, several stepchildren, grandchildren and great-grandchildren.

A traditional Native American memorial mourning walk will be held at 11 a.m. Thursday beginning at the Nichols Farm Cemetery on Shelton Road in Trumbull.

Aurelius Piper Sr., 92, Paugussett Tribe Chief, Is Dead

By The Associated Press
Aug. 12, 2008

TRUMBULL, Conn. (AP)   Aurelius H. Piper Sr., hereditary chief of the Golden Hill Paugussett Indian Tribe, died on Aug. 3 at the tribe's reservation in Trumbull. He was 92.

His death was announced by tribal officials.

Mr. Piper, known as Big Eagle, was named chief in 1959 by his mother, Chieftess Rising Star, and later assumed responsibility for the tribe's quarter-acre reservation in Trumbull.

Though small, the tribe, which has small reservations in Trumbull and Colchester, has been recognized by the State of Connecticut for more than 300 years. In 2004, however, the Bureau of Indian Affairs rejected the tribe's request for federal recognition.

In the fight to be recognized, the Paugussetts filed claims to more than 700,000 acres of land, setting off a flurry of legal challenges. The land claims, which stretched from Middletown to Wilton and from Greenwich through lower Westchester County in New York, were eventually dropped, but could have been revived if the tribe had received federal recognition.

In 1993, Mr. Piper's son Kenneth, also known as Moonface Bear, was the central figure in a 10-week armed standoff between state police and the Colchester faction of the tribe, over the sale of untaxed cigarettes on the reservation. Kenneth Piper died in 1996.

Mr. Piper traveled the world as a representative of the Golden Hill Tribe, Native Americans and other minority groups.

He served on many boards and commissions throughout Connecticut, fighting for the rights of American Indians and other minorities. He also served as a spiritual adviser to Native Americans in prison.

Mr. Piper served in the United States military during World War II, and took part in the troop landings in North Africa, according to the tribe.

He is survived by his wife, the former Marsha Conte; five children; and several stepchildren, grandchildren and great-grandchildren.

БИБЛИОТЕКА "МИР ИНДЕЙЦЕВ"

Книга IV

Клод Клэйтон Смит

ЗЕМЛЯ СЕРДЕЧНЫХ МУК

МЕЖДУНАРОДНЫЙ ЦЕНТР
"ТРАДИЦИОННЫЕ КУЛЬТУРЫ И СРЕДА ОБИТАНИЯ"

"TRADITIONAL CULTURES AND THEIR ENVIRONMENT"
INTERNATIONAL CENTRE

1994 г.

The hardbound edition of *Quarter-Acre of Heartache* that Chief Big Eagle inscribed to Alexander Vashchenko was stolen and had to be replaced, so the Russian edition was not published until 1994, the same year as *Red Men in Red Square.*

Shoran "Waupatukuay" Piper, Clan Mother of the Golden Hill Paugussett tribe, poses during an interview with *The Shelton Herald*. Ned Gerard photo, Hearst Connecticut Media.

CLAUDE CLAYTON SMITH, Professor Emeritus of English, Ohio Northern University, is the author of eight books and co-editor/translator of four. His own work has been translated into five languages, including Russian and Chinese. This is his fourth book with Shanti Arts. He holds a DA from Carnegie-Mellon, an MFA in Fiction from the Writers' Workshop at the University of Iowa, an MAT from Yale, and a BA from Wesleyan. He lives in Madison, Wisconsin, with his wife of forty-eight years. For further information, visit his website: claudeclaytonsmith.wordpress.com.

SHANTI ARTS

NATURE • ART • SPIRIT

Please visit us online
to browse our entire book catalog,
including poetry collections and fiction,
books on travel, nature, healing, art,
photography, and more.

Also take a look at our highly regarded art
and literary journal, *Still Point Arts Quarterly*,
which may be downloaded for free.

www.shantiarts.com